The Corporation
Under Siege

Risk

CONTROVERSIES

The
Corporation
Under
Siege

EXPOSING THE DEVICES USED
BY ACTIVISTS
AND REGULATORS IN THE
NON-RISK SOCIETY

*MARK NEAL
AND CHRISTIE DAVIES*

THE SOCIAL AFFAIRS UNIT

British Library Cataloguing in Publication Data
A catalogue record of this book is available from the British Library

ISBN 0 907631 77 0
ISSN 0966 2243 10

Book production and typesetting by Crowley Esmonde Ltd
Printed and bound in Great Britain by St Edmundsbury Press Ltd

Contents

Preface and Summary

During the early 1980s it was common to read of attacks on several industries because their products or by-products involved alleged hazards. In particular there were attacks on the tobacco industry, the alcoholic beverages industry and the pharmaceutical industry. By the 1990s the list of industries and products allegedly presenting some risk to health, the environment, the consumer, animals or the developing world had grown enormously. It now includes the huge farming and food industry, forestry, mining, water, chemicals, toys, tampons − everything 'from baby milk and Brent Spar to soya and silicone'.

In addition, two huge new 'industries' have emerged. Both, interestingly are totally unregulated. One consists of the activist groups attacking these products and processes in the name of claimed scientific findings and demanding regulation. The second is state and international regulatory agencies. The second is clearly a phenomenon worth attention in its own right. Do we want this huge extension of government and bureaucratic activity?

Dr Mark Neal and Professor Christie Davies chart the explosion in the sheer number of industries under fire. They go on to examine the way activists use and abuse science in such attacks. And they find that the same manoeuvres or 'devices' are used with many different products and processes. For example there is the 'cluster fluster' which involves finding clusters of a disease or problem in one particular area and then concluding that this is suspicious, as for instance in the cases of nuclear plants and electricity transmission wires. In reality, distributions are nearly always 'lumpy', for clusters occur naturally and spontaneously. Or there is 'the denial of dosage', where it is argued that because large amounts of X are dangerous, small amounts must also be harmful, as, for instance in arguments concerning pesticides. In fact large amounts of anything tend to be dangerous, and small amounts of a substance which is toxic in large doses can often be safe and even beneficial, as is the case with alcohol.

The practical consequences of their study are important. For the journalist, politician or member of the public confronted with an allegedly scientifically-based hazard they provide an inventory of questions to ask of the activist's use of science. Has he 'claimed a false consensus'? Scientists often disagree. This is inconvenient for the activist. So he cites sources selectively to suggest that a consensus exists. Or has he 'appealed to nature and purity'. Here the 'natural' is portrayed as benign and inherently good, even though untamed nature has been the greatest threat to the human race.

Neal and Davies go on to ask how it is that this obsession with risk has arisen in a society which is so long-lived, healthy and safe. They answer that modern science's ability to reduce and predict risk has opened the door to the 'risk agitators' finding potential risks which are in truth extremely remote or non-existent. Finally they add what I think is a genuinely original point about the non-reflexive nature of modern society. Supposedly established risks are rarely revisited in the light of new evidence. Once regulations are in place they stay. 'A murderer may take his case to appeal many years after conviction, why not a pesticide or a medicine?'

While the views expressed in this report are those of the authors, not those of the Social Affairs Unit, its Trustees, Advisers or Director, I warmly commend it as a spur to public debate.

Digby Anderson, 1998

1

Attacks on products: from baby milk and Brent Spar to soya and silicone

The cost of unjustified attacks on products and processes

One of the odder aspects of contemporary society is the way in which the providers of a product, especially if it is based on the use of a new technique, are liable to be subject to attack. We are particularly interested in those unjustified attacks which involve devices such as the dubious manipulation of words, images and statistics. Sometimes the attack comes from one of the eco-health-safety sects, and sometimes from a regulatory bureaucracy. Either way it may be a costly and damaging experience for the business concerned, which is forced to unravel the devices and to provide an elaborate and expensive refutation of the attack. For a small business the result can be bankruptcy and/or unemployment for its employees. For its customers it may mean having to pay a higher price for the product as a result of regulation, or it may mean being deprived of it altogether. The use of health, safety or green devices to malign or ban a product can mean ruin for the victims.

Such a phenomenon calls for an explanation and we will provide one in two stages. First, we will assess in a series of brief case histories some of the most common verbal and statistical devices employed and show how the same fallacy or misleading image may be employed time after time against quite different products.

Secondly, we shall consider why it is that modern western societies such as Britain, Canada, Germany and the United States, where life for most people is safe, healthy and relatively risk-free, are so liable to techno-moral panics, so over-regulated and so prone to eco-millenarianism. It is only by considering this social background that we can understand why these devices work at all.

The devices used to generate techno-moral panic

Anyone who engages in a trade, industry or profession is today at the mercy of three increasingly powerful, often heedless and even malicious groups: activists, regulatory bureaucrats and speculative litigants. These groups are commonly in search of money or power, or of that curious sense of satisfaction that is derived from the creation of a techno-moral panic[1] in which the public is frightened by recently-discovered dangers, and blame and opprobrium are pinned on some suitable target. The target is often a product, a marketable pleasure or a particular corporation, the very sources of the wealth of modern society.

In this section we are concerned with the devices that are habitually employed by those who seek to create, amplify and orchestrate such a techno-moral panic. Sometimes they are consciously employed. On other occasions they merely reflect the limited intelligence and unlimited prejudice of the panic-creators. Such devices take many forms. They may be devices in the use of words and images that divide the world into demons, innocent victims and bystanders, and heroic demon-slayers. Needless to say, the 'us' – crusading activists – are depicted as heroic and disinterested, and the 'them' – large corporations – as anonymous, malign and profitable. Other devices include the linking of dubious and sometimes mendacious 'facts' in ways that are irrational or unreasonable. Often the nature of both the 'facts' and the arguments is statistical;[2] the employment of quantitative data in this way merely adds an extra layer of mystification to an already murky story. These devices of rhetoric, fact and logic may be employed to mislead a court of law, to entrench the power of bureaucrats or to encourage supporting activists, and increasingly they are used to create media sensations through the manipulative use of press releases and the skilled provision of vivid and misleading images.[3]

In studying, describing and explaining the devices used against products we have chosen to proceed empirically by first citing a series of case histories based on recent controversies, indicating in each case the particular devices employed. On this basis it is easy to show that there are systematic patterns to the devices employed. The rhetoric turned against biotechnology[4] works, or rather misworks, equally well against mammifery silicone.[5] The pattern of the misportrayal of Nestlé over the sale of infant formula milk in developing countries[6] provides a template for the misportrayal of Shell over the disposal of the Brent Spar.[7] The misuse of arguments based on statistical clusters is common to campaigns against nuclear power stations[8] and to campaigns against the electricity transmission lines which also link generators fuelled by coal or gas.[9] There is method in their mendacity.

Furthermore the case studies we have chosen are only a reasonably representative sample of a much larger range of instances that we could have cited. Toys, fireworks, paper and packaging, cellular phones, calcium channel blockers, vitamins, tampons, guns, computer games, contraceptive pills, sugar and sugar substitutes, food additives, coffee, alcopops, and T-bone steaks – the list is endless – have all been subject to attacks that employ the devices we have sought to expose. But first, let us consider some case-studies.

Unnatural mice: the case of biotechnology
Biotechnology involves the development of genetically-modified organisms (GMOs) with recombinant DNA techniques, a technique commonly known as gene splicing. Since the early days of agriculture man has been concerned with the alteration of the genetic constitution of plants and animals through selective breeding. However, the new techniques of biotechnology are notable in that instead of relying upon the vagaries of reproduction, they are based on the direct manipulation, insertion or removal of

genes that determine particular characteristics of the organism. As this enhances our ability to design in, or out, desirable or undesirable characteristics, biotechnology has the potential to transform those industries that have the most direct impact on human welfare: agriculture and medicine.

Certainly, its role in the future of agriculture will be significant. Already, biotechnology has produced the 'flavr savr' long-life tomato as well as superior soya beans, insect-resistant maize and other cereals. Likewise, in the field of medicine, biotechnology now offers the possibility of using animals to grow human tissue, and organs such as livers, kidneys and hearts for transplantation. The techniques of biotechnology can also be used to produce insulin, haemoglobin and other human products from animals. Such developments will in time dramatically improve the quality of life of millions of people. Not surprisingly, though, both the methods and the potential products of biotechnology have proved to be extremely controversial, and they have been met with resistance in various forms, from moral criticism, to an irrationally high level of government regulation and interference, and the violent sabotage of institutions employing such techniques.[10]

Confusing process and product

Common to these various forms of criticism and opposition is a central confusion that muddles regulators and is exploited by agitators: the confusion between process and product.[11] At present, genetically engineered products are not fundamentally different from their counterparts produced by other means. A long-life tomato containing genetic material from fish is still a tomato. The super-chicken of tomorrow with its stronger legs, greater egg-laying capacity, greater resistance to salmonella and thicker egg-shells will still be a chicken. On the other hand, the dog breeders who long ago gave us the dachshund and the pekinese have fashioned monstrosities that fail in many respects to function as proper dogs, yet no-one has accused them of producing unnatural monsters. Likewise, it is difficult to see why the Cambridge 'Geep' (a GMO that is a cross between a goat and a sheep) should be any more shocking than that useful but sterile hybrid, the mule. Finally, it should be noted that the species boundary between humans and animals was breached long ago by Seventh Day Adventist doctors who in contravention of their sect's prejudices tried to transplant a baboon's heart into a human baby. Very few people objected. Why should it be any more controversial to ensure the success of such cross-species operations by cultivating truly human hearts in the bodies of animals? It is necessary strongly to stress this *continuity* between traditional and biotechnical methods of gene manipulation, because of the far greater (almost obsessive) degree of regulation of the new methods by bio-luddite governments in Europe.

The general tendency of supervisory bureaucracies to regulate processes rather than products, even though it is the products that impinge upon human life and the environment alike may be seen in an extreme form in the Directives of the European Union. As Henry Miller observed, commenting in 1997 on the then current European approach to Genetically Modified Organisms:

> ...in much of Europe where oversight has focused on GMOs, regulatory burdens have had substantial negative impact. The EU's directives 90/219/EEC and 90/220/EEC are focused upon GMOs and thus, are blatantly process based. The directives encompass both contained uses (fermentation in closed systems for producing amino acids, vaccines, or antibiotics for example) and planned introductions (that is, field trials or commercial uses outside containment of organisms such as plants, insects and animals). The EU itself and certain nations within it – Germany and Denmark especially – are widely perceived to have created potent regulatory disincentives to the use of new biotechnology.[12]

How excessive regulation hampers research and patenting

One consequence of these absurd and unscientific regulations is that Europe now lags way behind the United States in biotechnology research and production. This is reflected in the number of companies operating in the two continents. The United

States has over 1,300. Europe has only about 485. The United States holds 65 per cent of the world's biotechnology patents; Europe as a whole has only 15 per cent. Furthermore, research and development expenditure on biotechnology is three times as great in America as in Europe.[13]

The worst excesses of over-regulation and luddite violence are, not surprisingly, to be found in Germany, although Denmark and the Netherlands do not lag far behind. In Denmark, for instance, it is not permitted to take out patents on genetically-modified organisms; in Germany and the Netherlands there is considerable agitation to follow the Danish example, using the meaningless and emotive slogan, 'No Patents on Life'.[14] In Germany even academic researchers are trapped and strangled by regressive regulations. The German government has insisted that every single experiment is reviewed on a case-by-case basis, even where the risks are negligible.[15] Furthermore the problems for researchers are compounded by the aggressive activities of violent green hooligans, which the German government seems impotent – perhaps deliberately impotent – to restrain. Again the situation has been well described by Henry Miller:

Of some 6,000 field trials worldwide of plants genetically engineered with recombinant DNA techniques, only a few dozen have been performed in Germany. It is particularly disturbing that in 1995 all 15 of such small-scale field trials conducted by universities and research institutes in Germany were partially or completely destroyed by activists, even though most were studying the environmental safety of growing genetically-manipulated plants in normal agricultural environments. One postdoctoral fellow was attacked with stones while trying to protect his virus-resistant sugar beets from vandals … The vandals are abetted by governmental ambivalence and policies that equate innovation with risk. There is an obvious solution – one that has been purposely ignored by policy makers in both the EU and Germany: simply apply scientific and risk-based regulatory policies to the testing of gene-spliced plants ... Government regulation of field research with plants should focus on the traits that may be related to risk – invasiveness, weediness, toxicity and so forth – rather than on whether one or another technique of genetic manipulation was used.[16]

Officially labelled? – Irradiated foods

The same sets and kinds of criteria can be applied to the controversial question of food labelling. The government should label food in such a way that consumers are enabled to protect their own health and safety, but should under no circumstances go beyond this. Diabetics need to know whether a food contains sugar; those with a heart condition may be on a special diet; people with particular allergies need to be vigilant about what they eat. However, there is no reason to suppose that any greater risks are attached to genetically-engineered tomatoes, cornflakes or chickens than to their so-called 'natural' equivalents.[17] Specifically to label genetically-engineered foods would be contrary to the needs of health and safety, for it would drown out and confuse necessary health information by the addition of irrelevant 'noise'.[18] It may well be that food sectarians will wish to add peculiar labels of their own to food depending upon their particular esoteric ethic. There is no reason why they should not be permitted to do this, in much the same way as the Beth-Din decides whether particular items of food are *kosher* or *traife*, or whether they are suitable for a meat, or for a milk meal.[19] However, it is no business of the state to enforce, encourage or foster labelling of this kind. Indeed, it is in the public interest for the government strongly to discourage the labelling of genetically engineered, or, come to that, irradiated food.

Process not product: the broader context

The absurd restrictions on the development and use of genetically-modified organisms in Europe reflect the mind-sets both of activists and bureaucrats; neither group is willing to address the complexities and uncertainties of the real world so they substitute campaigns against, and the regulation of, particular easily discernable processes such as genetic engineering rather than trying to assess any potential problems associated with its products. In the case of the activists the row over biotechnology has been in many respects a re-run of the panic over irradiated foodstuffs. To treat food in this way to kill off bacteria is an eminently sensible way of protecting the consumer against food-poisoning but it is anathema to greenists, who are less concerned with the safety of the product than with attacking the process that made it safe. The difficulties of decision-making are thus replaced by crude and simplistic symbolic politics.

The confusing of process and product that we have discussed in relation to biotechnology, irradiated food and pasteurisation is partly the result of the fears and superstitions of the ignorant. People who are capable of believing that they have been abducted by little green beings from outer space[20] or that there is Satanic ritual child abuse in the Orkneys (in each case in the absence of any evidence) are hardly likely to be able to assess the risks associated with the products of biotechnology or irradiation. They are far more likely to assert that we have here processes that are mysterious and sinister and which should be regulated regardless of the level of risk posed by the products. The German protesters who mounted a *pogrom* against their scientists' impure and abominable genetically-modified sugarbeet are best seen as savages who live in a peculiar moral and intellectual universe, one haunted by demons disguised as vegetables who can destroy everything. Nothing else can explain their irrational destructiveness and their stoning of the scientist who had committed adultery against nature.[21] The German police, as is traditional on such occasions, have done nothing serious to detect, prosecute or imprison these violent hooligans. Presumably they too are trapped in the same bubble of irrational fear of demonic vegetables.

You can't see it but you can see the clusters: nuclear power and electricity transmission cables

People are afraid of radiation. Radiation is invisible, invasive and immaterial and can cause that most feared of diseases, cancer. The high incidence of cancer in the early workers with X-rays, and among those exposed to the radiation generated by nuclear explosions long ago revealed that radiation can be deadly.[22] Electromagnetic fields are equally invisible, invasive and immaterial. Perhaps in consequence they have also been suspected of causing cancer.[23] Very similar techniques have been used to create techno-moral panics in relation both to nuclear power plants and electricity transmission lines. The first stage is to search for clusters.[24] If the incidence of any disease including cancer is plotted on a map, clusters will inevitably be found, even if the disease is randomly distributed.[25] By chance some of these clusters may be found close to a nuclear power station, or an electricity transmission line, but it may well not signify anything at all.[26] The clusters that cause the greatest alarm are leukaemia clusters, leukaemia being a form of cancer that, unlike most other cancers, afflicts children.[27] For the propagandist this is an exploitable situation, for an innocent, powerless victim has been struck down at a young age with a serious disease, something that is otherwise rare in a modern society with a very low incidence of child mortality. The existence of such victims calls out for somebody to blame, preferably a large corporation such as one of the nuclear or conventional electricity generators or an armaments manufacturer.

One of the most recent sets of cluster fusses occurred in the Newbury area in England in 1997. In the first cluster case to be considered here, activists alleged that there were levels of plutonium in the soil around the Aldermaston Atomic Weapons Establishment and around the Greenham Common air-base in excess of the usual background levels, resulting from distant causes such as the atmospheric testing of nuclear weapons by the Chinese. Whether there really was such an excess or whether it was an artefact of changes in the methods of measuring such contamination is uncertain but the levels were low and unlikely to affect people's health. However, predictably, one of the activists also found a leukaemia cluster and proclaimed: 'These results (the levels of radioactivity found by the local survey) are highly significant and certainly should be considered in any investigation on excess leukaemia around Greenham Common which we know exists.'[28]

Meanwhile on the other side of Newbury, well away from the alleged sources of radioactivity, there was another political clash over a leukaemia cluster. Members of Newbury District Council attacked Berkshire Health Authority for its alleged inactivity in the matter and outlined, 'a strategy to try to pinpoint a cause of the south Newbury leukaemia cluster'.[29]

It doesn't seem to have crossed the good councillors' minds that *there may not have been an overall cause at all*, merely a set of individual cases, each with its own separate and complicated pattern of causation. The only person who seems to have grasped this point was a local senior environmental health officer who commented: 'In studies the only correlation between leukaemia and environmental criteria was the location of fire hydrants.'[30] However, the councillors, whose concern was entirely under-standable, if misplaced, determined 'to meet with their opposite numbers in Northampton where there [was] another unexplained cluster of leukaemia cases'.[31]

By linking up in this way, the towns' representatives may well have turned these local campaigns into a national or even inter-national one. At a slighly earlier date, another local newspaper, *The Northampton Chronicle,* had 'discovered' a leukaemia cluster on a Northampton council estate and a certain Pembroke Road became 'in the language of Fleet Street ... the "Street of Doom"'.[32] As Jolyon Jenkins put it, 'the area's prospective Parliamentary candidate (now MP), Sally Keeble, took the families to lobby at the House of Commons. Lawyers circled. If it felt like everyone knew their part in this script, perhaps it was because it's been performed so often before'.[33]

Precisely so. Cluster hunting and cluster agitation has become a standard part of the political culture not just of Britain but of other western democracies, sometimes with serious, sometimes with humorous consequences. As Mark Mills observed:

One intriguing study of clusters of diseases was performed in the United Kingdom. The analyst found clusters of a specific cancer in the vicinity of military installations. It turns out that the installations were medieval castles. The author of the study (a statistical expert) had simply searched for a disease that clustered around a selected set of physical locations. Careful selection of time, space and events can create such clustering for all diseases and events.[34]

The need for a suitable villain to blame – the defence industry

Whether a particular piece of cluster bluster blows over or persists probably depends on whether it is possible for the agitators to round up one of the usual suspects. The Northampton and South Newbury agitations may well subside in time because of a failure to identify someone to blame. Recalcitrant health authorities that refuse to waste taxpayers' money on expensive surveys that they know will reveal nothing are not a good target for a long campaign of agitation. They are too closely associated with the virtuous regulation of public health. By contrast leukaemia or other disease clusters which can be pressed into a spurious association with radiation or electromagnetic fields may form the basis of a protracted agitation.

The Aldermaston weapons plant could well be subjected in the future to a lengthy and well-organised hostile propaganda attack. Public fears of radiation and of electromagnetic fields, being irrational, are easily amplified by a media panic. Part of the reason for these fears is that both radiation and electromagnetic fields are invisible and thus mysterious. Since people cannot by themselves directly gauge their nature, their magnitude or their effects, they are reliant upon other sources of information, sources that are all too often unreliable and sensational. Also, many find it difficult to believe that the bulk of the radiation to which they are exposed (nearly 90 per cent) comes from natural sources and that most of the small dose of artificial radiation that they receive comes from the medical use of X-rays.[35] Most natural radiation is unavoidable and the careful use of X-rays saves far more lives through earlier and more accurate diagnoses than it destroys through stimulating the development of cancer.[36] Green activists living in a house built on granite (and possibly built of granite) with a deep cellar and energy saving double glazing and draught excluders are far more likely to die of radiation-induced illness than those who live next door to a nuclear power station. Radon gas emitted by the granite will percolate into their energy-efficient house and the very devices they have used to prevent heat escaping will also corral the radioactive radon gas inside their walls where they will be forced to breathe it.[37]

Visible risks, invisible costs
One of the main factors in explaining the effectiveness of the panics stirred up by agitators in respect of radiation or electromagnetic fields is that the risks (such as they are) are far removed from the everyday dangers that people feel able to confront and master. In consequence, it is easy to deceive people by providing an exaggerated estimate of the level of risk involved. By contrast, people are often blasé about the more direct physical risks associated with the so-called renewable sources of energy. All dams whether used as sources of water or of electricity carry some risk that the dam will burst, sweeping everything before it in a great surge of water. Despite this, people continue to live downriver from dams, and to ignore or tolerate the risks associated with them. A dam is a solid, secure object, and may have survived for decades. Even though the risks associated with radiation are much lower than those involved in the collapse of the dam, it is the former that are the subject of scare stories and propaganda.

However we choose to manufacture and transmit energy, there will be risks associated with it. There have always been explosions in wind and water mills, and catastrophes happen in coal mines all around the world. In the case of the relatively trivial risks associated with nuclear energy and electricity transmission, any attempt further to depress these risks will incur substantial costs. Indeed, the lower the level of absolute risk involved, the greater will be the marginal cost of producing any further improvement.[38] It would be very costly for example to bury major power lines underground, let alone to try to neutralise the electromagnetic fields in people's houses caused by their own domestic electrical wiring and appliances. This cost would have to be met by an increase in electricity prices which would result in a fall in electricity consumption. In addition to the negative effect this would have on quality of life, there would no doubt also be increased fatalities from hypothermia, or due to the elderly groping their way down the stairs in the dark. During the twentieth century, the consumption of electricity in the advanced industrial countries of North America, Western Europe and the Far East has increased enormously, as has the amount of electricity transmitted down power lines. Curiously, the inhabitants of these countries seem to be living longer than ever before. Health goes with wealth.[39]

Writing melodrama I: innocent children at the mercy of infant formula baby milk

Baby food has for years been a controversial issue.[40] For many radical health activists, particularly those of a third-worldish tinge, the ultimate villain is – or at least was – Nestlé which had committed the ultimate crime of selling powdered baby milk to mothers in poor countries, who would then use it as a substitute for their own maternal milk. Not only was this seen as depriving the infant of essential nutrients and antibodies, but there was also the risk that the mothers would make up the milk using polluted local water supplies, and would thus transmit infectious diseases to their offspring.

Rarely has a bogus health-scare drama had such a strong cast. In the role of villain was a large, anonymous, profit-making multinational company; whereas the victims were that most sacred of all combinations, the human mother and child. Needless to say, the plot also featured other crucial dichotomies such as the benign 'natural' versus the malign 'artificial' and the oppressive, exploiting West versus the innocent, Third World. It was of no avail to point out to the health activists that in many cases the mothers were malnourished and unable to provide their children with sufficient milk, nor to indicate that the packets stated very clearly in a pictorial as well as a written form that any water used in making up the infant formula should be boiled first.[41] The health activists were neither willing to concede that Nestlé were acting in good faith, nor that the Third World mothers had good and rational reasons for using Nestlé products. Indeed, reading health activists one often wonders whether they credit consumers with having any capacity for rationality whatsoever. Their implicit contempt for the Third World female consumer is little short of racism.

Far from being a source of insidious marketing techniques, Nestlé have consistently subscribed to the 1981 WHO code on the marketing and distribution of powdered baby milk.[42] The false allegations against Nestlé made by the healthist radicals were to the effect that in practice Nestlé ignored the rules and regulations laid out in this code. IBFAN, the International Baby Food Action Network, in a wide-ranging and much publicised report, alleged that Nestlé had broken the WHO rules in no fewer than 455 instances.[43] Not surprisingly, this gained a good deal of press coverage, and, no doubt, was believed by those with a prejudice in favour of whistle-blowing health activists, who are wrongly perceived as being accurate because they are equally wrongly perceived as being disinterested. As a response to these accusations, an independent committee was set up which included representatives of WHO and UNICEF to investigate the entire situation. Out of the 455 allegations only three were upheld by the committee, and one of these had already been dealt with before the publication of the IBFAN 'report'.[44] However, the refutation did not enjoy anything like as much publicity as the original smear. The undermining of bad news isn't news.

Writing melodrama II: save our sea
A very similar pattern underlies the 1995 Brent Spar controversy involving Shell and Greenpeace. In 1991, the Brent Spar, a floating oil storage and loading facility owned by Shell, came to the end of

its operational life. A series of investigations and discussions took place to seek the best practicable environmental option for its disposal, and in 1994, commissioned experts came out in favour of deep water disposal in the Atlantic Ocean.[45] In February 1995, the British Government agreed to this and informed other European governments of its decision. In April of that year Greenpeace told the world's press that the Brent Spar contained over 100 tonnes of toxic sludge, and over 5500 tonnes of oil.[46] Next, Greenpeace activists occupied the Brent Spar claiming that deep water disposal would set a precedent for getting rid of 400 other oil rigs in the same way, and that this posed a major threat to the marine environment.[47] This illegal act triggered off violence by sundry green *sturmtruppen* (stormtroopers) in Germany, who fire-bombed Shell petrol stations in an orgiastic *Tankstellenacht* (night of the filling-stations). For some reason or other Germans have a tendency to express their rage at events in other countries by destroying local property, presumably to the grief of the German insurance companies who have to pay out. Chancellor Kohl, responding courageously to these events in his own country, begged John Major, the then British Prime Minister, to find an alternative way of disposing of the Brent Spar. By 20 June 1995 Shell had had enough and agreed that it would choose some other means of disposal, even though dismantling the Brent Spar on land was and is less environmentally friendly than deep water disposal.[48] Subsequently, it has become clear that Greenpeace's statements concerning the pollutants that would be dumped in the ocean together with the Brent Spar, were grossly inaccurate.[49] In particular, the amount of oil contained in the rig was only 100 tonnes, rather than the 5,500 tons claimed by Greenpeace – ie less than two per cent of the Greenpeace figure.[50] Indeed the evidence was so damning that, on 5th September 1995, Greenpeace UK apologised to Shell for their crass error in estimating the amount of oil that would be left on the rig. At last the Greenpeace campaign was exposed as a media victory over truth.

Activism as big business: Greenpeace

It was also a victory for 'disguised' big business over overt big business. Greenpeace may have the appealing image of a group of anorak-wearing amateur enthusiasts pursuing whaling ships on rubber rafts. Yet Greenpeace already had earnings of over $30 million per annum in 1993-94.[51] It is a big, rich organisation in the large and growing green pressure industry. Greenpeace has also proved adept at using its considerable financial resources to manipulate the media. In the Brent Spar case alone, Greenpeace spent a great deal of money recording and transmitting television images from a video-editing suite set up on the Spar during their occupation.[52]

It is clear in retrospect that radio, television and newspapers alike relied far too heavily upon the Greenpeace side of the story because it made good copy. They failed to give equal prominence to the careful scientific studies done between 1991 and 1994 on the different environmental impacts of the different modes of disposing of Brent Spar.[53] Greenpeace *has to exaggerate* because that is the only way in which it can maintain its size and importance. In the competition for green support, green funds, green enthusiasm and green judgement it is the green organisation with the slickest slogans that comes out on top. For example, at the time of the Brent Spar controversy, Greenpeace took out a full page advertisement in a national newspaper in Britain that stated, 'If you let Shell have its way, it'll soon be the only shell left in the North Sea'.[54] No doubt this false claim alarmed shell collectors from Kirkwall to Kent, and the further false claim that poisonous chemicals from these rigs were going to damage all marine and human life created yet further shell-shock. This was, however, not the only Greenpeace advertisement to prove misleading and inaccurate, for the advertising standards authority (ASA) condemned and forced the withdrawal of one of its parallel high profile anti-nuclear advertisements.[55]

Crusades against progress

It would be unfair to suggest that Greenpeace and other

greenpeacers are simply indulging in the cynical and mendacious manipulation of public opinion. Rather, there is every reason to think that they really do believe their own nonsense. Activists of this type are not concerned with selecting the least bad of several options in an inevitably imperfect world. Rather, they are crusaders against modernity for whom the fate of the actual environment is subordinate to the pursuit of strongly held symbolic goals. This ultra-green attitude has, perhaps, been best expressed by one of Greenpeace's rivals, David Gee, formerly the director of Friends of the Earth UK, who said in support of Greenpeace after the Brent Spar farce, 'The incident has established the moral principle of "not dumping at sea" over the narrower technical "best practicable environmental option"'.[56]

It is very difficult to see why the adoption of a more environmentally harmful procedure should be regarded as establishing a moral principle. What Mr Gee's extraordinary claim reveals is that he does not live in our ordinary human world of risk, cost and balance, but in a world of metaphysical absolutes where the pure and sinless sea may not be sullied in any way, even if this means creating far greater problems on land. In the discourse of many of those who espouse such irrationality may be discerned a primitive pagan belief system in which the earth and the sea are treated as if they were themselves both sacred and human. Those who adopt such an ideology use science when it suits them, but only in an opportunistic way and in a context that is strongly anti-scientific.

Purity and danger: how Eurocrats pass our water

Water is, as we have seen above, pure and sacred. It can baptise away sin and cleanse a Brahmin polluted by an unspeakable contact with an Untouchable. Believers in its essential purity are even outraged at the thought of harmless quantities of fluoride being added to their drinking water to protect children against caries and hence tooth-ache. True believers may even choose to drink water from a drain-pipe filled wooden water-butt, or a private well dug into a dubious aquifer, rather than imbibe the chlorinated water from their taps. If by chance their natural water supply happens to contain sodium fluoride to an extent that mottles their teeth, or traces of lithium salts which inhibit depression and aggression, homicide and suicide alike, this is acceptable; but should such substances be added, even accidentally, to their drinking water by some human agency this is cause for outrage.

It is not surprising then that in the 1980s our European regulators decreed almost homeopathic maximum acceptable concentrations of such agricultural chemicals as herbicides and pesticides for the drinking water of EC countries. Indeed they have set the levels of maximum concentration almost as low as the limits of the measuring instruments used by the chemists who check the purity of the water. For all intents and purposes it was a surrogate for zero.[57]

The absurdity of the proposed Europurity rules can be seen when they are compared with the guidelines issued by WHO as shown in the table below.

TABLE ONE[58]

Agrochemicals	EC Drinking Water Directive MAC in µg/l	WHO Guideline value in µg/l
Aldrin	0.1	0.03
Dieldrin	0.1	0.03
Atrazine	0.1	2
MCPA	0.1	2
Molinate	0.1	6
Isoproturon	0.1	9
Alachlor	0.1	20
Pendimenthalin	0.1	20
Bentazone	0.1	30
Pyridate	0.1	100

What is immediately apparent is that the Maximum Approved Concentrations (MACs) put forward in the EC Drinking Water

Directive that were first promulgated in 1980 were the same for all 10 of the key agrochemicals listed. It is highly unlikely that all 10 of them should have been equally hazardous, and an inspection of the corresponding WHO guideline values at the time indicates that this rival group of would-be regulators perceived the chemicals as differing widely in their potential toxicity. In eight of the 10 chemicals listed the maximum concentrations permitted by the WHO guidelines were higher than those of the Eurowater directive. It is clear that the single uniform Eurofigure for the MACs was determined not by levels of risk but by an obsession with bureaucratic order (one Europe, one directive, one maximum allowable concentration!) and a wish to appear super-environmental. The MAC levels for the same chemicals in comparable and competitor countries such as the United States, Canada, Australia and Japan were set higher and more realistically by reference to the findings of toxicologists.[59] The health and longevity of their populations do not seem to have been impaired by this trust in science rather than bureaucratic rhetoric.

The mechanistic regulation of complex systems: perverse side effects of regulation

The mechanistic approach of the bureaucratic regulators to questions of water quality fails to understand that the use of agrochemicals is not an arbitrary, wanton debauching of the environment by Europeasants egged on by multinational chemical companies but rather one part of a diverse set of technical and economic decisions. If European farmers are forced to desist from using optimum quantities of herbicides, pesticides and fungicides to protect their crops this will have knock-on effects, not simply for the agricultural and chemical industries and for the consumer whose food will become more expensive, but even for the landscape. Ecological over-regulation in one area of life can produce ecological damage on a broad scale because of the regulators' failure to understand the nature of complex technical and economic systems.

Farmers forced to cut back on herbicides will tend to intensify mechanical means of weed control by buying new, heavy and expensive equipment that can only be used effectively in larger, more manageable fields. The British hedgerows and the French bocage that are the delight of the rambler, the blackbird and the foxhunter are already in danger from Eurosubsidised mechanisation and would soon disappear if hard-pressed farmers substituted machines for pesticides or for environmentally friendly, genetically-modified crops. The movement of such heavy equipment across the fields would also result in soil compaction and, in time, a loss of soil fertility. The diversity of crops sown at present in Europe which makes rural Europe so much more pleasing in appearance than say Saskatchewan or Kansas depends on the flexibility that the farmer gains from having available a rich diversity of agrochemicals appropriate to particular crops and circumstances. If, due to over-regulation, many of these cannot be used, then farmers will be forced to switch to a crude, onesided, unbalanced agriculture that keeps them within the tramlines of Euroregulation.

Writing melodrama III: mammary mummery – the case of silicone implants

One of the more salient panics of recent years has concerned the case of silicone-gel filled breast-implants.[60] By the 1980s, the manufacturers of these products had become somewhat too relaxed about possible future panics. Implants had been on the market for over 30 years, and there was little public concern about their safety. There was therefore thought to be little need to sponsor research into their health risks. Towards the end of the decade, however, cases arose where women successfully took the manufacturers of their implants to court. The women claimed to be suffering from various disorders, which their lawyers assigned to the women's artificially-enlarged breasts. Even so, the complaints at the time did not particularly alarm the leaders of the industry, who in 1990 took reassurance from a survey commissioned by the American Society of Plastic and Reconstructive Surgeons, which found that over 90 per cent of women were happy with their implants.[61]

The situation, however, changed dramatically when the American President George Bush appointed David Kessler as the new commissioner of the powerful American Food and Drug Administration (FDA). Kessler's credentials were impressive, but he was a zealot when it came to public health and safety issues, and he soon suffused the FDA with radical health activism.

The new zeal-filled FDA's attention was soon drawn to the court cases against the silicone implant industry, and it seized the chance to enter the fray. The accusations that the complaining women made against the manufacturers differed widely in terms of symptoms and conditions. Some of the problems were well-known: one being the hardening of the breasts caused by scar tissue; another being the fact that up to five per cent of the implants leaked.[62] What the complainants and the FDA needed, however, was a new theory that would integrate these disparate symptoms into one unifying 'syndrome'.

Bans and regulation on the basis of unproven hypotheses

The FDA then held a series of enquiries expressing concern about silicone implants, and eventually issued a ban on them in 1992, saying that the manufacturers had not adequately demonstrated their safety. The ban was, like many such bans, promulgated badly, such that it was widely interpreted as official confirmation that silicone implants were indeed harmful and dangerous.

Behind the ban lay a widespread, though unproven, belief about the effects of silicone on the auto-immune system; the reinforcement of this belief by the ban meant that women with implants were now inclined to blame any disorder from which they suffered on their implants. There was, consequently, a wild stampede by jittery American women to have their breast-enhancements removed. In one case, a woman who could not afford the operation even attempted to take her implants out with a razor blade.[63]

The arbitrary FDA ban was also seen as a go-ahead for litigation, and thousands of women took the manufacturers to court for a variety of usually irrelevant, unrelated ailments. These legal actions were often successful, and spectacular sums were awarded on the basis of very weak evidence. However, in the absence of any real epidemiological studies, the industry found it impossible to disprove even the more ridiculous allegations, such that by 1994 the manufacturers were forced to settle a class action, collectively stumping up in total the vast sum of $4.2 billion. A notable feature of this settlement was that around $1 billion out of this sum was set aside for the payment of the lawyers' overheads. This fed a scramble for 'victims' and there was a consequent spate of advertising campaigns on both sides of the Atlantic. The corresponding UK feeding frenzy is well described by Celia Hall, under the headline 'Breast Implant Damages Sought by 10,000 women':[64]

> An estimated 10,000 British women are hoping to win damages in the American courts for harm allegedly caused to them by silicone breast implants. The deadline by which they must register in America for a share of the $4.2 billion global "no liability settlement" is Thursday of next week. The Law Society in London confirmed yesterday that it had processed 5,000 claim forms. Another 2,000 have been handled by two firms of UK solicitors, and a total of 300 other British solicitors are handling at least one claim each.

Why these products were so vulnerable

Silicone implants were a health scare waiting to happen. The Western cultural preference for big breasts had led thousands of women in the United Kingdom and millions of women in the United States to have large masses of a synthetic gel stuffed inside their bodies, indeed within their breasts – those universal and potent symbols of motherhood. Apart from the various forms of heart devices, such as pacemakers, silicone implants were the most widespread, and the largest, manufactured parts ever to be inserted into women's bodies, and left there for many years.

With many health scares people can trim and alter their

behaviour to avoid contact with whatever product is the current demon-of-the-week. People can decide not to go near nuclear power stations. They can choose not to eat red meat or food containing additives. They can stop drinking alcohol, or give up smoking. They can request a change of treatment from their doctor if there is a techno-moral panic about a particular form of medication. In each of these cases, people can immediately alter their lifestyle to accommodate the latest fad. They feel that they have some semblance of control.

By contrast, the silicone implants lay sealed within the women's bodies, encased in the very breasts they enhanced. The implants had thus become an integral part of their owners as well as being visible features of them. Once the panic had set in and the highly questionable auto-immune theory had taken root, the frightened women's choice of an active response to the situation was restricted to one thing: to have them removed. Whereas avoiding other demonised products usually concerns relatively minor and reversible choices such as cutting out beef, cutting down on saccharin or sugar, or buying environmentally 'friendly' detergents, avoiding 'the risks' associated with silicone implants involved a major and painful operation.

Once it was established by the courts that implants were for legal purposes 'dangerous' it was understandable that whereas very few women had suffered from any related health problems before the late 1980s, now they were associating them with all kinds of conditions from stomach cramps to myopia; the implants were used to straddle and connect all manner of diffuse symptoms and conditions. A hypothesis duly emerged and firmly took root, regardless of the fact that it was just that – a hypothesis. It was claimed that the silicone implant caused or encouraged the development of 'connective tissue' diseases – which took in all kinds of common conditions, notably rheumatoid arthritis – and that they adversely affected the body's auto-immune system. Proposing such a link between silicone and the auto-immune system, albeit on the basis of very little evidence, opened the floodgates for litigation, as everything from migraines to swollen ankles could now be blamed on the implants. File your claims now, *mesdames, faites vos jeux*. The putative link between silicone implants and connective tissue disease exploded into the public consciousness in December 1991, when the manufacturers were sued for several million dollars.[65]

This was not just American-style litigation. It was understandable that once women were alerted to the fact they might be harbouring a dangerous technology within them, that they should be alarmed about possible symptoms of harm or of damage being done to them from within. Thus a combination of hyper-vigilance, misdiagnosis and avarice was at the heart of the panic.

Later, after the suing women, the lawyers and the surgeons had pocketed their cash and departed, a new factor in this drama arrived late at the scene: hard research findings. The safety studies initiated earlier as a response to the lack of information about silicone now began to produce results, and these results showed that far from being a sinister gel within, silicone implants were actually relatively safe. The research to date is still continuing and is far from conclusive but one conclusion *can* be drawn from it, namely that the FDA-generated panic about a 'lack of information about safety' had led to the banning of products that were safe. As Marcia Angel observed:[66]

At the time of the ban on breast implants, David Kessler acknowledged that there was no evidence that breast implants caused connective tissue disease. He simply felt he could not wait for the evidence to be assembled before banning them. For their part, the courts had long since decided that implants caused connective tissue disease. Now, years later, the evidence is beginning to emerge. We are beginning to see that any connection between implants and connective tissue disease is likely to be very weak at most, since several good studies have failed to detect it. Given the absence of scientific evidence at the time, why were the courts so sure of their conclusions?

The results: unemployment

As always, the people who were the losers were those who worked for the manufacturers. Health activists are quite happy to see industries sued to the point of extinction, and many of their activities tend to encourage this. What they forget in their pursuit of the 'public good', is that group words like 'industry' or 'company' disguise and render anonymous ordinary people who themselves have health concerns, families to support and mortgages to pay. The assumption that making companies pay does not harm people is not only wrong but dangerous. The class action payment of $4.2 billion meant in practice that those whose work was directly or indirectly related to the silicone implant products either became unemployed or suffered financial loss. Furthermore, it meant that investment by these industries had to be restricted, and that those people who would have benefited from such investment in terms of jobs or career, did not. It meant a shedding of staff, and ruin for many people. So here the invisible victims of a techno-moral panic – ordinary working people, who, unlike the healthist agitators, are voiceless and would not be listened to anyway.

Politically correct and politically necessary: finding innocent bystanders

It is a characteristic of certain kinds of junk science that their findings can be predicted on sociological grounds long before there is even a whiff of evidence. The politically necessary but scientifically untenable findings are sure to follow. A classic example of this is to be found in the prescient musings about tobacco of the sociologist Peter Berger, long before the current panic about passive smoking,

> ... some years ago I made a prediction. I mention this with pride, since social scientists rarely make predictions that come true ... I said that the anti-smoking movement had a big problem, at least in Western democracies. Even if smoking were as harmful to smokers as was claimed the natural response would be to call it a matter of individual choice,

33

and to resist calls for regulation. "If I want to kill myself", the argument would go, "that's my business. The Government should protect others against me, but not me against myself."

The only solution to this problem available to the anti-smoking movement, I said, would be for it to find – and this was my term – an "innocent bystander". I suggested that one means of doing this would be to convince people that they could be harmed by the smoking of others.[67]

Needless to say, a vast quantity of research has been done into the effects of passive smoking,[68] some of which has satisfied the not very demanding criteria of accuracy favoured by health activists. However, the results of the studies that purport to show that the inhalation of other people's tobacco smoke causes lung cancer have proved fallible in two stages; this does not of course mean that these studies will cease being quoted by enthusiasts for 'health correctness'.[69]

Relative risks and absolute risks

Two of the first generation of studies of environmental tobacco smoke (ETS) seemed to indicate that there was an increase of about a third in the incidence of lung cancer among non-smokers exposed to other people's smoke, relative to non-smokers not so exposed.[70] These apparent results were given enormous publicity by anti-smoking healthists everywhere and in Canada the government ordained that cigarettes and cigarette advertisements should warn the world that 'Passive Smoking Causes Cancer'.[71] What the healthists did *not* tell the public was that the incidence of lung cancer among non-smokers was low and that the absolute (as distinct from relative) extra risk incurred by those seen to be most likely to be exposed to passive smoking (the spouses of smokers) was trivial.[72] However, to make sure that everybody got the 'undiluted' message about the fatal consequences of passive smoking, the American Environmental Protection Agency (EPA) stated that, 'the widespread exposure to environmental tobacco smoke in the United States presents a serious and substantial environmental health impact.'[73]

It is now clear that even the claim of relative risk of lung cancer from passive smoking postulated by the anti-smoking industry may be dubious.[74] Many of the studies of the effects of environmental tobacco smoke have not shown any significant increase in the incidence of lung cancer among those exposed to other people's tobacco smoke.[75] The two main sets of early studies showing a significant increase in risk, namely those done by Trichopoulos and his colleagues,[76] and those carried out by Hirayama[77] have been savagely criticised by statisticians to the point where they no longer possess any credibility.[78] Despite this they are still cited without any apology or disclaimer, by health and environmental activists.[79]

Two recent surveys of the studies[80] of the effects of passive smoking have further pointed out that the epidemiological studies in general are flawed, and contain biases that require correction. In particular, smoker misclassification has produced a spurious association between spousal smoking and lung cancer.[81] In plain language, some of those classed as being the non-smoking spouses of smokers had been either secret smokers or had forgotten their sinful past as smokers; their development of lung cancer should have been ascribed to their own indulgence rather than to the harmless environmental smoke wafted across from their spouses. When allowance is made for all these defects in the studies cited by the anti-smoking agencies, it is clear that the increased absolute risk to non-smokers from passive smoking is either non-existent or very small indeed.[82] Rather than divorcing a smoking spouse on health grounds it would make more sense to eat an apple.

2

Why are modern societies so prone to scaremongering about environmental and health risks?

A typology of devices

What is striking about the devices used by bureaucrats or agitators, or both, is how repetitious they are. A device played against one product is sure to turn up again and be used against another. For convenience we have assembled various devices in the Table on pages 38-41.

From the table it is clear that the same devices are used time and time again. The fluster about clusters which has been wheeled out against the nuclear industry is also part of the campaign against power lines. The idea that nature is sacred and must not be interfered with that has been employed against genetically-modified organisms is used in the same way against the irradiation of food. None of these arguments are profound for they employ clearly and obviously fallacious devices and our refutations of them are based on commonplaces available to everyone. There is nothing mysterious or difficult involved. However, knowing this only raises a further and more intractable problem – why are such devices so successful? They certainly are successful as we can see both from the harm and the cost that many of the devices described in the text must have inflicted on a variety of products and from the fact

TABLE TWO

Name of Device	How it works	Examples
1. Initial Exaggeration of Hazard	Exaggeration gets headlines. Even when claims are later reduced, challenged, or abandoned some of the original mud may well stick. Later evidence that challenges or disproves exaggerated and alarmist claims tends to get much less media coverage than the original irresponsible allegations.	1 *Alleged dangers of infant formula baby milk.* 2 *Assessment of the oil in Shell's Brent Spar rig* 3 *Risk of diet-related disease.* 4 *Risk from alcohol.* 5 *The Alar apple scare.* 6 *Asbestos in schools.* 7 *Calcium channel blockers.*
2 The Cluster Fluster	This involves finding clusters of a disease or problem in one particular place, and identifying this as abnormal or suspicious. In reality distributions are nearly always 'lumpy', for clusters occur naturally and spontaneously. They are not in themselves evidence of a health or environmental 'problem'.	1 *Leukaemia and other cancer clusters around nuclear plants or military installations.* 2 *Scares over electrical transmission wires and cancer.*
3. Coincidence equals causality	The coincidence of a particular 'risk' factor with a negative health or environmental outcome is often treated as hard evidence of a causal relationship.	1 *Scares over drugs, such as those concerning Opren and Nifedipine, and other calcium channel blockers.* 2 *Scares over Prozac*
4. Stressing relative risks while ignoring absolute risks	The actual chances of suffering harm from many hazards are very low. This awkward fact can be concealed by using devices such as playing up the relative risk and showing that those who use a product are X times more likely to suffer harm than those who do not. This sounds impressive and makes good headlines. The actual absolute chances of harm remain very low, but that is rarely	1 *Environmental tobacco smoke.* 2 *Various contraceptive pill scares* 3 *Toxic shock syndrome and tampons* 4 *Calcium channel blockers*

Name of Device	How it works	Examples
	mentioned, for low absolute risks do not make good headlines.	
5. **The Denial of Dosage**	It is often argued that because large amounts of X are dangerous, small amounts must also be harmful, though on a smaller scale. In fact large amounts of anything tend to be dangerous, and small amounts of a substance which is toxic in large doses can often be safe, and even beneficial.	1 *Agrochemicals* 2 *Pesticide and weedicide residues* 3 *Water quality* 4 *Artificial sweeteners* 5 *Asbestos* 6 *Food additives* 7 *Radiation*
6. **Devices with words and images**	These include the familiar, 'Up to as many as 20 million people may be at risk of …', the use of doctored photos to shock, the cutting out of the ifs and buts normally associated with science, the portrayal of consumers as naïve innocents, companies as malign conspiracies and health and environmental activists as selfless heroes. It also involves the artful suggestion that all things new are risky, and the old is safe	1 *Anti-biotechnology scares* 2 *Brent Spar* 3 *Assorted anti-pharmaceutical scares* 4 *Anti-meat campaigns* 5 *Campaigns against hunting and against nuclear power.*
7. **Harm minimisation that ignores pleasure and benefit**	Many products can be harmful for some consumers, or even third parties. It is not, however, legitimate to add up these costs as part of an indictment while ignoring the pleasures and benefits for which they are purchased and used. A low risk world is not necessarily an optimal one and harm minimisation can lead to tedium and misery.	1 *Alcohol* 2 *Tobacco* 3 *Cars* 4 *Fireworks* 5 *'Unhealthy' foods* 6 *Irradiated foods* 7 *T-Bone steak* 8 *Anti-hunting campaigns* 9 *Anti-roads campaigns*

Name of Device	How it works	Examples
8. **Claiming a** **false consensus**	Scientists often disagree. This is inconvenient for activists. The device is to cite sources selectively so as to suggest a consensus exists. Alternatively collections of old studies get added together to create a new collective 'meta' study. Sometimes the statistics from the individual studies are illicitly added to create a big pseudo-sample.	1 *Passive smoking* 2 *The extent to which man's activity is responsible for global warming and for the hole in the ozone layer and what the consequences will be.* 3 *The extent of the acid rain problem and the degree of harm it causes.* 4 *What the 'The Healthy Diet' is.* 5 *Deer hunting – whether the deer experience excessive suffering.*
9. **The appeal to** **nature and** **purity**	Nature is portrayed as being benign even though untamed nature has been the greatest threat to the human race. Environmentalists and healthists alike use this crassly sentimental appeal of the natural as good and the artificial is bad.	1 *Infant formula baby milk* 2 *Campaigns against agro-chemicals* 3 *Food irradiation* 4 *Silicon breast implants* 5 *Nuclear power* 6 *Pharmaceuticals* 7 *Artificial sweeteners* 8 *Anti-road/runway protests* 9 *Brent Spar* 10 *Biotechnology* 11 *Food additives*
10. **Sentimentalising** **the victims:** **protecting** **innocent** **children**	Activists divide the world into innocent consumers and bystanders, and greedy corporations. The most innocent of all are children, and the most powerful rhetoric is concerned with protecting them. In real life, children need to learn incrementally to take risks and exercise judgement as they grow older.	1 *Environmental tobacco smoke* 2 *Infant formula baby milk* 3 *Hand guns* 4 *Computer games* 5 *Snack foods* 6 *Toys* 7 *Fireworks* 8 *Food additives*

Name of Device	How it works	Examples
11. Omitting the costs and dangers of regulation	Those who want products regulated stress the dangers of the product, but are rarely able to show that the regulation will work as intended. Nor do they investigate or measure any costs the regulation may have, such as, for instance, their impact on employment. Yet regulations can be ineffective, costly and have major negative effects. Excessive pharmaceutical regulations keep healing and pain relieving drugs out of the patients' reach. Activists can not foresee the exact effect of a particular regulation. It would make more sense to demand that the regulation be implemented for a trial period, so that its efficacy and cost could be assessed. The unscientific nature of contemporary activism is shown by the fact that they rarely do so.	*1 Alcohol* *2 Pharmaceuticals* *3 Meat industry* *4 Egg producers* *5 Regulation of NHS dentistry* *6 Franchising of legal aid and solicitors* *7 Biotechnology*
12. Demanding the impossible	After a product has been shown not to be unsafe, the agitator demands that it be proven to be safe. The best that can be done is to prove a low level of risk. Agitators demand a perfect solution where in the real world of necessity we have to choose between solutions offering different patterns of costs and benefits, none of which are perfect. Agitators may even rule out the least costly and least harmful of these because they insist that some irrational absolute criterion be adhered to.	*1 Silicone breast implants* *2 Pharmaceuticals* *3 Brent Spar* *4 Biotechnology* *5 Nuclear power stations*

41

that they have been used time and time again. Some are even re-runs of much older and earlier campaigns.

Thus, when it was first decided to pasteurise milk in the nineteenth century, a process now regarded as routine, safe and necessary, many objections were put forward against it, such as: heat destroys great numbers of bacteria in milk and thus conceals evidence of dirt (purity and danger argument); pasteurisation would lead to an increase in infant mortality (the most innocent of victims argument); and it is wrong to interfere in any way with Nature's perfect food (intervention in nature is dangerous).[1] However, so far as is known, there were no reports of tuberculosis clusters in the vicinity of dairies supplying pasteurised milk to local customers.

It is, in a way, reassuring to find that our ancestors were just as foolish and gullible as we are, but nonetheless the reckless use of devices to try to undermine the reputation of a product does seem to have increased. Our ancestors lived in a real 'risk society', where everyday life was menaced by the very real risks of infectious disease or sudden accident. By contrast, we live in a 'trick society' where everyday life is far less hazardous but where we may be mentally ambushed at any turn by the devices of agitators or bureaucrats and falsely told that we are at risk. The key questions we must ask are: 'why are we so susceptible to devices?'; 'why are more used now than in the past?'; and 'what is it about our modern societies and their institutions that makes it so easy to mount such attacks on reputable products to produce a techno-moral panic?' The answers to these questions lie in the nature of modern society, the 'device society' that has replaced the risk societies of the past; in the massive growth of controlling bureaucracy which, in Britain and in Europe, accelerated in the 1980s and 1990s; in the muddled way in which we receive information from the mass media even when the media-persons are being honest and well-intentioned; in the rise of a bizarre, almost sacrilegious veneration of nature[2] and a corresponding rejection of modern technical achievement by jaundiced eco-activists, the yallery-greenery brigade; and in the peculiar and distorted way in which we now perceive guilt and blame. We shall deal with each of these factors in turn and show how they have helped to create the unbrave new world in which the devices are used.

Modern society is long-lived, healthy and safe yet prone to risk agitation

Modern society is by any standard of comparison far less risky than any in the past. People in most parts of the world live longer than ever before and are less likely for any given age group to suffer a crippling injury or a chronic illness. Our failures are those of success, for as we live longer, and are more likely to survive serious insults to the body, so too our real enemies, namely time and nature, the forces of ageing, provide us with new forms of deterioration, pain and debility. Mortality is a long and unpleasant business, not risky but certain.

The risks we face today, unlike those of the past, are very much visible ones. In the past, the plague or smallpox could decimate a population, killing as much as a third or a half of the people and no one had any idea how it was caused. In a world that knew nothing of parasites, bacteria or viruses, let alone prions, disease could be irrationally declared to be a divine punishment for sodomy, the result of witchcraft or caused by the Jews poisoning the wells. At a time when people lacked any secure grasp of modern scientific notions of cause and effect, there was always an unknown and unknowable catastrophe coming tomorrow and the characteristic response was to round up the usual suspects in an outburst of finding someone to blame. Malaria was seen as an ague associated with a miasma from the marshes, and the idea that it could be caused by a parasite transmitted by mosquitoes would have been regarded as being as absurd as the suggestion that plague came with fleas that travelled on rats.

Today we may worry about the decreasing effectiveness of anti-malarial drugs or the long-term effects of using DDT, but at least we know the broad parameters of our most immediate problems and we know how to acquire new knowledge and new techniques. Risks are no longer unknown, invisible and mysterious in the way that they were, even in the mid-nineteenth century when it was difficult to convince people that cholera outbreaks in London were due to an infected water supply.

Yet our very success in reducing and predicting risks has created classes of people who make it their business to magnify risks and to invent new ones.[3] We may term them risk bureaucrats and risk agitators. The greater our powers of measurement and pseudo-measurement, the further we seek to understand complicated situations involving the interaction of a very large number of factors, the more scope there is for campaigns against products, products that are by any ordinary calculations harmless.

Modern society is non-reflexive: we don't learn from our mistakes

Also modern societies, though rational in a technical sense, are not what we now call 'reflexive'.[4] It was possible for our Victorian ancestors to abandon tradition, often with great personal anguish, but their descendants are in general quite unable to challenge the rigid assumptions of their own way of life even though it is crumbling into crime, illegitimacy and addiction due to the contemporary inability to manage blame properly. Those in positions of power are unwilling, and perhaps unable, to be openly sceptical about the dominant alarms concerning health, pollution or the environment, or to challenge the ruling principles that govern regulation. Reflexivity is out. In particular there is an unwillingness to go back and reconsider the toxicity and dangers of products that have been banned in the past and to reinstate them if further testing and the passing of time reveals that they are to all intents and purposes harmless.[5] A murderer may take his case to appeal many years after conviction; why not a pesticide or a medicine? It is in all our interests that accurate chemical justice be done, for we all pay the cost of excluding a useful product by regulation and thus of being forced to switch to a more expensive or noxious substitute. Besides, the very essence of science is replication. Just because one test, or one set of tests, many years ago seemed to indicate a danger, it does not follow that there was

44

or is one; to tie oneself to the uncertain state of knowledge at some arbitrary point in the past is absurd, yet that is what legal regulation does.

Scares once established are not periodically reassessed

The problem is a very broad one, for when many of the great scares of the past – saccharin, asbestos in buildings, benoxaprofen, acid rain[6] – are revisited, the threat turns out to have been negligible or even non-existent, or one of much lesser magnitude than was alleged at the time. But those who live in the agitational-regulatory culture rarely look back, repent or recant. The baseless campaigns of the past are still seen as part of the heroic march towards greenery and public health, when even a minimal degree of reflexivity would cause the perpetrators to look back at their own errors and amend their present thinking and procedures.

The mark of a truly non-reflexive institution or society is its inability to reverse or revise its beliefs or procedures, even when it has become widely acknowledged privately that they are nonsense. The planned economy of the Soviet Union under Brezhnev-Andropov-Chernenko provides an example of this. The Common Agriculture Policy of the European Community is another such disaster. Those who design and implement such policies are locked into them and feel compelled to go on pursuing and justifying them, even though they sense that they may lead to disaster. It is in this sense alone that we can speak of an institution as being non-reflexive (or, conversely, reflexive). Only individuals within institutions can think; institutions can't. When we speak of an institution or a society as being reflexive, all that is usually meant is that one section of it has the ability and autonomy to assess and criticise an otherwise dominant view, such that even the adherents of the old view are forced to reconsider their position. In a non-reflexive institution, such as the regulatory agencies of Germany and North America, this is impossible. Both at the level of basic assumptions and at that of everyday technique, they are, for both political and bureaucratic reasons, unable to 'reflect' on their own inadequacies.

The most basic of these inner absurdities, which the regulators are unable even to contemplate revising, is the precautionary principle, the idea that regulators must always lean to the side of caution at whatever cost. Arthur Flemming, the then Secretary of the American Department of Health, Education and Welfare, put a version of this doctrine to the US Congress, declaring that a responsible government must make public health its top priority 'even though by so doing it may be acting against the economic interests of a segment of our society'.[7] Flemming totally failed to ask any questions about how probable or serious the risks to public health were or, what were the costs that the regulations imposed on a mere 'segment' of society. He preferred to go for cheap but in the long run expensive rhetoric.

The cranberry scare

Flemming was the man who pulped America's cranberry crop just before Thanksgiving because it contained traces of the weedkiller aminotriazole, which the US Food and Drugs Administration, on the basis of very dubious evidence indeed, had decided might be carcinogenic.[8] The farmers were inadequately compensated and the manufacturer lost the possibility of selling a profitable line in weedkillers. What was never contemplated by Flemming was the possibility that the cost in human lives and human well-being caused by the new regulations might greatly outweigh any possible benefits. Bankruptcy, a sudden anomic loss of income or social and economic position or being forced to comply with irksome regulations can lead to suicide, stress-related illnesses and death, and to the generally higher morbidity and mortality associated with poverty.[9] It is perhaps not surprising that (male) farmers are one of the occupations having the highest suicide rate in Britain.[10] Isolation and excessive regulation would seem to be the probable causes, giving a combination of egoistic and fatalistic suicide;[11] certainly farmers themselves have been known to cite the burden of the regulations imposed on them as a source of stress that could have led to their colleagues' suicides.

Deaths due to over-regulation

Yet the deaths stemming from over-regulation are seldom recorded or measured, even when jobs, businesses and livelihoods are being suddenly wiped out by decree, and we never get to know whether the probable deaths caused exceed the possible lives saved. This shrinking of our concern to the unknown persons whose lives are allegedly saved by a health or safety rule is a curious inversion of our usual preference for saving the lives of particular known individuals over those of mere statistical persons.[12] Normally we are more concerned to protect the lives of the members of a small known group at risk, rather than those of an anonymous mass of people, yet farmers in America are forced to use relatively dangerous pesticides such as organophosphates because the safe ones are believed to convey (unproven) long-term dangers[13] and the owners of small British abattoirs are driven out of business by increased regulation because health and safety regulators put their welfare below that of unknown 'statistical' persons. They are treated as a mere economic 'segment' of society. Yet in the long-run we are all at risk as the effects of over-regulation slow down the growth of the economy and undermine health and well-being generally. The American analyst Ralph Keeney estimated in 1990 that if a regulation costs $7.5 million per supposed life saved then it will also cause an equivalent degree of loss of life from impaired living standards,[14] yet these indirect costs of regulation are ignored. Products continue to be victims, and so do people. Wildavsky's comment about the United States may well apply to other countries too when he says 'The current method of risk assessment and regulation makes people sicker in the name of making them healthier'.[15]

Products cannot be proved to be safe: it is silly to demand they are

Part of the problem stems from the widespread insistence that a product be *proved to be safe*. It is quite impossible to prove that any product is safe; at best one can say that it has not been demonstrated to be substantially unsafe or that it seems to be safer than its substitutes. There is no such thing as a safe, risk-proof world. Anyone who claims that 'we must ban a product because it has not been proved to be safe' is out of touch with reality, but that is what happens in a non-reflexive society full of *haute-couture* petty emperors.

Anything in too large a dose or concentration is harmful or poisonous. Even the selenium so favoured by health food addicts would damage them in larger doses. Yet fears about drugs or additives or agricultural chemicals or atmospheric asbestos regularly lead to the irrational assumption that because a substance is harmful in large quantities that it must also be dangerous at minute doses. A standard test for whether a chemical is carcinogenic remains that of stuffing a hapless rodent with enormous quantities of it (the 'maximum tolerated dose') and waiting to see what happens. It is by its very nature a highly unreliable predictor of the effect on human beings of the ingestion of tiny and occasional quantities of the same substance.[16] Yet we go on using the test and both regulatory institutions and agitators prove obsessively resistant to the idea that there might be a 'safe' dose, and that below a certain threshold a substance can be effectively harmless.[17] Rather they demand proof that such a threshold exists even if there is no positive evidence that low doses are harmful. Such proof is by the very nature of things impossible and so societies remain locked in a grid of irrationality. It is one more proof of the absurd lack of reflexivity in western society where questions of risk are concerned.

None of the criticisms of risk-thinking that we have made above are obscure; most of them are commonplaces and rather obviously true. However, such criticisms cannot be conceded by, say, the regulators of North America or the agitators of Europe, as it would destroy much of the rationale for what they do. Both groups are purveyors and consumers of junk science and they dare not think too hard about the untenable assumptions and dubious procedures on which their science is based. It is better not to reflect on such matters, and not to ask the wrong kind of questions about the behaviour of one's own institution or group.

Unwillingness to reconsider condemns arthritis sufferers to keep on suffering

Even in cases where the regulators do behave in a sensible and balanced way, other factors can promote rigidity and irreversibility within society. Once, for example, a safe drug has been withdrawn due to agitation, there is little chance that it can ever be brought back, even if the alternatives are less efficacious and have harmful side effects. There are, for example, not enough effective anti-arthritic drugs, yet two of the key ones have been removed from the market.[18] The story is well told in *Living with Risk* :

The use of PEM (prescription event monitoring) has already demonstrated how misleading media reports on drug effects can be. One example is the short history of the anti-arthritic drug *Opren* (benoxaprofen). In January 1982 it became headline news after eight cases of jaundice had been associated with its use by 6,000 patients. Early follow-up showed that at least five of these cases had nothing to do with the drug, but it was nevertheless removed from the market in July 1982. Inman's team then reviewed, in detail, a total of 24,000 patients who had received *Opren*, finding only one case in which the drug could probably be blamed for causing jaundice, and that was non-fatal. Another 11 cases were possibly connected. Thus the side effect was truly very rare, and the risk of fatal jaundice immeasurably low, if it existed at all. But following such bad publicity, it would then be impossible to re-introduce the medicine, however great its benefits.

Another anti-arthritic drug, *Zomax* (zomepirac), was withdrawn in the US and Britain after a small number of reports of fatal allergic reaction (anaphylactic shock), one patient being related to the owner of a television network and his illness thus generating vast publicity. There is an existing risk (for all people, all causes) of anaphylactic shock of about one in two million. No death of this nature occurred among patients taking *Zomax* in Britain. The PEM study showed that patients on the drug had a lower risk of death overall, being in some way protected from coronary thrombosis and stroke. And this effect was quite independent of the markedly beneficial pain-relieving effect of the drug, particularly in patients with terminal cancer. But because of gross misuse of risk-related information, the drug is, essentially, gone for ever. And its apparently beneficial effect on the circulation can never be properly evaluated. Irresponsible journalism can be responsible for much suffering.[19]

In this case, the irreversibility was achieved not through the crass rules and biases of a bureaucracy but through the blinkered way in which risk scares get covered in the media. A product can be killed off by agitators and journalists and there is no way of reviving it. Were production started up again and the drug re-marketed under a different trade name, the facts would soon be revealed and there would be a new witch-hunt on the theme 'the public's right to know'. In fairness many journalists probably would behave in a self-critical way and the better-informed ones would denounce the scare-mongers. Even some of those who had previously attacked the drug would realise that they had been deceived last time (much as journalists were angry at being grossly manipulated by Greenpeace over Brent Spar) and would now defend the re-issued drug. The media after all is a highly varied and differentiated institution with as many sensible folk as scare-mongers. Nonetheless the scare-mongers would win simply by creating enough doubt and uncertainty to revive the original tarnishing of the drug's reputation. Such is the power of a tiny minority of irrational troublemakers to destroy a product through the creation of a techno-moral panic.

3

Bureaucrats, Greens and Greenocrats

Bureaucracy: playing safe

The enforcement of safety regulations by bureaucrats is not necessarily about safety, but may well be more concerned with potential criticism or litigation. As the Americans say, it is all about 'covering your bureaucratic ass'. Regulations are structures to hide behind when things go wrong. In a disaster brought about by a failure of judgement or character by the bureaucrat, it can always be pleaded that 'the correct procedures were followed', even if this actually contributed to the disaster.

Defensive bureaucracies would, for example, prefer a total ban on biotechnology, or, failing that, a set of regulations that constrain all GMOs within a new set of stringent regulations that are not applied to the more haphazard products of traditional breeding or the risky procedure of moving an old species to a new geographical area. It isn't about risk, then. It is about blame. The committees that have strangled Europe's biotechnology industry in green tape are afraid to make decisions based on a scientific judgement of the overall risks of releasing, or even just producing, a particular GMO, as compared with the risks associated with the species and associated techniques that will be substituted for it if it is banned. If they ban the particular GMO and there is in consequence an economic or an ecological disaster, they will nonetheless escape blame.

However, if the same regulatory bureaucrats allow the GMO

to be developed and employed, and there is an 'official enquiry', it will be no defence for the committee to say, 'We used our judgement, intelligence, experience and scientific knowledge and made a rational decision about the relative risks'. Rather than be severely criticised and possibly lose their prospects of future perks and gongs, the bureaucrats prefer to *play safe* – not for the sake of the public, but for their careers. They prefer to regulate by process, not product,[1] because it fits their career strategy of defensive bureaucracy, of following rule books and precedents and avoiding real and realistic decisions.

Members of the professions are apt to support green causes and, perhaps without thinking, to sympathise with those who regulate by process, not product. After all, in theory, quacks and incompetents are eliminated from their own professions by the laws which declare that it is necessary to be qualified to practise as a lawyer, doctor or dentist or to be employed in a state school as a teacher. There is no need to worry about the product if it is guaranteed by the process of training and examining.

However, the members of all these professions have now become the subject of intensified governmental bureaucratic regulation, to the point where many of their members quit because they can no longer carry out their duties correctly and ethically as independent professionals. Mr M'Turk, a dentist who has recently left the NHS because of the escalating paperwork, told us that he did so because he had entered the profession to look after people's teeth, not to fill in endless dental patient plans justifying his every decision in writing to appease the government inspector. He had one patient who was under permanent instructions to phone up just before an appointment so that it could be cancelled if the inspector was there. The dentist had carried out treatment in the best clinical interests of the patient in a way that did not fit the inspector's schedule of what should be done. The patient was happy to agree since he was satisfied with the product; the inspector would, however, have penalised the dentist because he was concerned with process, a process that crassly assumed that there was such a thing as 'best practice', and which allowed for no differences of opinion or experience nor for variations in the nature of patients' preferences. Needless to say the bulk of the practice's patients have followed him into the private sector. They prefer quality to regulation.

Monitoring process rather than ensuring good products

A similar point may be made in relation to criminal legal aid work, an area where the government is faced with rising costs, as the members of a feckless underclass insist on committing more crimes. The problem could be solved by further restricting the availability of legal aid (or in another context, education). However, this would be electorally unpopular, so the government has gone for franchising, ie, placing cheap block contracts for legal aid work only with firms, partnerships or solicitors' chambers that satisfy certain peculiar conditions. Once again the emphasis is not on the product, ie, an honestly-gained verdict that the defendant was not guilty or at least could not be said to be guilty beyond reasonable doubt – result one satisfied client. Rather it is on process, on the routine completion of the case paperwork.

Thus a firm that employs no staff is still required to describe in detail its process of induction of new staff and this has to be checked and updated each year. Likewise a small firm consisting of people who know each other on a face-to-face basis is required to have an appraisal scheme. It is all irrelevant to the preservation of quality, and like most of these schemes discriminates in favour of the large firm. A large firm specialising in commercial law can employ a group of second-rate criminal lawyers on a hire-and-fire basis, pick up a franchise and absorb the costs of unnecessary regulation in its general administration. The service is lousy and the personal contact and continuity with clients is missing, but, when the franchise snooper comes round, all tick-boxes are correctly ticked. Such a mode of regulation doesn't work for the benefit of the public, but it can be used as a disguise for the lowering of professional standards and it is cheap to operate. The franchise snoopers do not require a proper legal training (which would make them expensive), or even a relevant degree; a couple of recent, devalued A-levels will do. In essence they are petty clerks whose sole skill lies in following a paper-trail through the files. They have no real understanding of the product they should be monitoring.[2]

Behind the meaningless dance of the regulatory bureaucrats controlling commercial-scientific and service-professional products may be seen the deceptive manoeuvres of the politicians. Faced with public concern at media stories about health and environmental risks, or declining professional standards following a cut in public funding or an expansion in client numbers, politicians rush to reassure the electorate lest they lose votes. The point of their activities is not to protect us against serious hazards effectively and efficiently or to maintain standards of service but, to use political jargon, to send the right messages: 'Something is being done'; 'You are being protected'; 'Quality is being preserved'. Whatever happened to acid rain or gold-standard A-levels?

It is important to make the connection between the regulation of those professions whose product is not sold in the marketplace but paid for by government, and the regulation by the state of new industrial and agricultural processes. In both cases the bureaucrats feel unable to measure the product but have to provide a reason for their own existence so they go for process. Ironically the members of professions suffering insane over-regulation by their government pay-masters are often prone to support an increased level of regulation in other areas such as biotechnology. It would be far more rational of them to join forces with the purveyors of genetically-modified organisms in a concerted campaign against bureaucracy.

Businessmen and professionals, scientists and consumers all have two enemies in common: the outraged mob, who are incapable of rationality; and the regulatory bureaucrats who pervert it. The members of both groups fail to understand the nature of products and vent their stupidity on processes. The present situation thus requires new political alliances and acts of vigorous defiance to force the politicians to curb the hooligans and restrain the regulators.

The myth of the good greenocrat

The victims of health scares, environmental excitements and regulatory offensives are at a disadvantage in rebutting allegations and smears because the public have often been deceived into thinking that bureaucrats and green activists are disinterested and truthful. They supposedly reflect popular sentiment and are thus in some sense democratic. By contrast entrepreneurs, innovators, manufacturers, marketers and advertisers are represented as only interested in profits and are, therefore, not to be trusted. Recent television coverage of green activists trying to stop by-passes and airport runways has shown loveable muddy-brown protesters in tunnels and treehouses, with green nick-names like Skunky or Feral, being battered into submission by plastic-helmeted security men. Such pictures only confirm the existing prejudice against those who make, build and do. The media were equally gentle with the green stormtroopers who impartially attacked petrol stations, nuclear transporters and genetically modified vegetables throughout Germany. Likewise stringent regulators with heads like light-bulbs and the outraged ostrich-faced expressions perfected on the screen by the late Richard Wattis are treated as sources of oracular wisdom and not subjected to the same kind of harsh cross-examination as the 'representatives of capitalism'.

Regulators have a vested interest in more regulation

Yet why should we regard the regulators as disinterested and truthful? Their careers, their salaries and their egos all depend on the extension and intensification of regulation. More regulation means a bigger organisation, more jobs, a broader span of control, a taller hierarchy of command, bigger salaries and more perks for those at the top. This is especially true for the employees of, and consultants to, international organisations, whose salaries are set at the level of the richest participating country, who pay no tax and enjoy luxury travel for trivial reasons. We are not criticising the regulators for being greedy or ambitious, merely saying their institutions should be restructured so that these human appetites will lead them in a more productive direction. Above the bureaucrats, of course, the lawyers wheel and hover in the sky. Their interest lies in having new and complex regulations that lead to protracted disputes, appeals and moves from one jurisdiction to another. Both bureaucrats and lawyers have a clear self-interest in new products being examined on a case-by-case basis at the expense of consumer, producer and tax-payer.

Beyond these lures lie the more dubious pleasures of power. The regulatory bureaucrat gains the perverse satisfaction that is only to be found in blocking someone else's projects. He is a thwart-hog. His is the joyous assertion of negative power, of *Kraft durch Schadenfreude*. It is all the more satisfying because these base emotions can be fused with an ideology of protecting the public. It is reasonable to compare their situation with that of the enacters and enforcers of Prohibition in the United States in the 1920s. Ah, the pleasure of putting a wealthy brewery out of action while enjoying the praises of the Women's Christian Temperance Union. In the background can be heard the sound of that early environmental activist, Carrie Nation, chopping down a bar with her axe.

Psychological satisfaction from activism

There is no valid reason for taking today's green hooligans' motives any more seriously than those of yesterday's teetotalist vandals. How wonderful to be able to commit crimes and behave in an anti-social way and yet have an inner sense of your own sanctity! What bliss to be able to depart from the complexities of our everyday life with all its uncertainties and enter a world of simple absolutes! Best of all is the joy of the individual who makes an irresponsible escape from an over-regulated world into green anarchy. It is an odd paradox that those environmentalists who have renounced regulation in their own daily lives and entered the order of the green Thélèmites should be such stern advocates of more state regulation.

In time most of the members of antinomian sects return to their original privileged or boring backgrounds. The Trotskyites of the 1970s are now newly laborious, and the green protesters of the 1990s will probably end up teaching environmental science, thus making life easier for the civil servants of the Department of Education who are trying to hide the fact that science teaching has collapsed in most state secondary schools. The more successful among the green protestors will become bureaucrats in the larger green pressure groups. Like the regulatory bureaucrats they will come to see their career prospects as tied to the size and power of their unproductive organisations.

The productive capitalists, small businessmen and self-employed people who are the victims of the mania for expansion of the regulators are likely to be far more democratic and far more truthful than either the bureaucrats or the greens. Many of them lack the size, the power, the resources, the political influence or the lawlessness to fight or defy their regulators. There is nothing stronger than the power of the state, that sole repository of legitimate violence, except the EGOs, the Eurogovernment organisations. Our fishing fleet, our abattoirs, our small cheese-makers and our beef industry have all been destroyed by Euroregulation in the name of health, safety and the environment. How could our small businessmen, farmers and artisans possibly fight against the unscrupulous power politics of Brussels, the politically loaded advice of the Euroregulators and the obsessional and unpatriotic zeal of the power-hungry British civil servants, to whom the task of enforcement has been delegated?

Unlike the green activists our businesspeople are law-abiding folk, although some sectors have been provoked to breaking point. Certainly, the Eurotreatment of British farmers has been a disgrace. Since 1996, beef farmers have witnessed the systematic destruction of their livelihoods through various levels of extreme anti-risk policies. The absurd banning of the T-bone steak in December 1997 was the last straw, and the Welsh farmers' celebrated Holyhead beef-burger party signalled the beginnings of British agro-radicalism.

Until then, only Europeasants had done that kind of thing, even though their local governments largely ignored the foolish edicts of Brussels. Our tradition of enforcing and obeying European law, even when it is an ass, has become a major liability.

When there isn't any evidence, regulate anyway

A good example of the new and increasingly powerful breed of healthist zealots came in the form of the former Canadian Minister of Health, M Marc Lalonde. His view on health matters was that the state regulators should not wait for solid evidence of risk before imposing increased regulations, or bans. This approach to public welfare matters became known as the Lalonde Doctrine, which stated even when evidence was uncertain and ambiguous, health messages to the public should be 'loud, clear and unequivocal'.[3] Fired up with this agenda the Canadian authorities forced the cigarette manufacturers to inscribe 'Passive Smoking Causes Cancer' on their packets even though there was no persuasive evidence that it did. The tobacco companies were simply not as powerful as the Canadian healthist lobby. Their scientists, like those working for the pharmaceutical industry, have to be far more scrupulously careful and truthful than the critics of the industry. If research has been sponsored, or paid for, by one of these industries then the moment the results are published, they will come under critical and sometimes mendacious attack if they do not conform to current healthist prejudices. The researchers must get it right first time. They cannot afford to make the kind of mistakes to be found in anti-tobacco or anti-pharmaceuticals research. Nor can they dare to exaggerate the importance or conclusiveness of their findings because they might be met with a chorus of 'Well, they would, wouldn't they?' They have no protective ideology to shelter under in the way that the Lalonde doctrine excuses and encourages the exaggeration and distortions of health activist researchers. Industry-sponsored scientists are honest precisely because they are not trusted whereas healthist-environmentalist scientists can afford to be careless and dishonest precisely because they are trusted.

The innocent distortions of the media: the environment in which devices occur

Those wishing to use devices against a product often seek to exploit the press, radio and television as a means of spreading their messages, and we have seen some of the devices that they use. However, the very ways in which people in the media put together words and images often helps the cause of the scare-mongers. Certainly, scare stories are news, whereas retractions that there is nothing to be scared about are not. The former get prominence, the latter are ignored or tucked away on obscure pages along with the critics of impending ecological doom scenarios. It is rather like a libel action that has been quietly settled out of court. The libel is remembered, the apology is largely unread.

Sometimes the media are simply irresponsible in the way they run such stories. They either use devices or allow devices to be used. However, even when journalists and newspapers behave completely responsibly and honestly, the conventional narrative structure of news stories can work against a product.

Consider for example the following innocent device-free news story, entitled, 'Honey not safe for young children' from a sagacious writer and reputable paper.[4] It begins, 'Honey, regarded as one of the purest foods in existence, has been declared unsuitable for babies. There are also fears that honey made from the pollen of genetically-engineered crops could endanger people's health.'[5] We have here a double-honey-whammer guaranteed to spoil the appetite of even Winnie the Pooh, that combines two quite separate honey stories that have nothing to do with each other in a single mellifluous but misleading one. Warnings now placed on commercial honey producer's jars say that honey should not be given to children under 12 months old as a precaution against infant botulism, for as a Ministry of Agriculture newsletter notes 'Very occasionally honey may contain low numbers of naturally occurring bacterial spores' which small babies' guts can't cope with'.[6] Fair enough, though why we have to be told the irrelevant information that 'honey is one of the purest foods in existence' or that the bacterial spores occur 'naturally' is not explained.

Honey is a gloriously sweet, soft and sticky food for which most of us would fight our way through a heffalump trap at the dead of night, but it is not at all clear in what sense it is any more pure than the highly refined chemical sucrose (sugar) that is fed to the bees in order that they may process it through their bodies to excrete honey. What makes honey exciting for structuralists and romantics is that it is both a food that may be found wild and raw in nature and one manufactured by the bee. In our present context it is possible that the term pure refers to a lack of such later human additives as beneficial flavourings, colourings, preservatives, etc. Even the threatening bacterial spores are described as 'naturally occurring' as if identical bacterial spores unintentionally introduced by some human agency would be more menacing. The words 'pure' and 'natural' here are mere conventional rhetorical decoration but they get in the way of our understanding. However, the real problem arises from the second scare story, where we are told that,

Botanists have found that bees can pick up mutant pollen from transgenic crops – crops altered to carry foreign genes – with potentially serious effects on human health. Millions of pounds have been spent over the past decade by companies "reinventing nature" – mixing plants' natural genes with others ... Some of these added genes are toxic to humans as well as insects, others can cause violent allergic reactions. Genetically-altered pollen "could pose problems to man who consumes honey as a food" says the study.[7]

Purity and danger
Why anyone should wish to consume honey other than as a food is not made clear. However, a familiar monster has been created by the sowing of genetically-modified dragon's teeth. The familiar phrases ring out: 'mutant pollen', 'foreign genes', 'reinventing nature'. The language of xenophobia has been crossed with that of science fiction to transform the beloved familiar honey of Pooh into a genetic nightmare version of the abstract honey that Jean-

Paul Sartre found so disgusting and presumably alien and nauseous.[8] We are given the further irrelevant information that 'millions of pounds' have been spent by companies on the genetic experiments. Thus it is big business that is to blame for the coming clover catastrophe.

The first stage of this classic narrative, one as bound by convention as an ancient folk-tale is of course shock-horror. Our old friend the busy little bee, industriously collecting our food for us from the fairest flowers of nature, becomes a source of poisonous excretions due to our human folly and hubris in planting genetically-modified crops.

The second stage is the familiar one. 'We must have regulations'. Predictably the leading researcher on the honey project is quoted as saying 'It is essential that genetically-modified plants are scrutinised very carefully before any release to take into account any potentially adverse effects on the environment'.

Finally, rather late in the day we get to the third stage, where the reporter gets the researcher to admit:

> there was no evidence that anyone had been harmed … What we were trying to do was to represent the worst-case scenario. [Currently] in insect resistant crops the proteins that have been produced are non-toxic to humans. They are highly specific to insects. The scenario we constructed is an extremely unlikely scenario, though there is still an element of risk.[9]

At last, the whole truth is revealed, namely that it isn't going to happen and there isn't anything to worry about. However, there is an 'element of risk', presumably comparable to the risk of a person who is severely allergic to bee-stings being murdered by a bee on a visit to the hives to buy honey, or of a pot of honey falling off the shelf on to the head of a person with a thin skull at a supermarket. It is of course possible that in the distant future someone may die of eating honey in a world of genetically-modified plants but that is no more a reason for regulating genetically-modified crops than for ridding our shops of all items that at present produce occasional deaths by allergy, from feather-filled duvets to peanuts.

Unfortunately, we have no guarantee that the reader got to the end of this thrilling bee-feature narrative and was reassured that the risk was remote; he or she may have chosen to select out and focus on the earlier and more exciting 'shock-horror' and 'time for more regulations' sections. There may yet be further scare campaigns directed both against the honey industry and against genetically-modified crops, set off like a tornado by a butterfly, by this innocent little story involving respectable journalists and academics. Yet if the very structure of habitual narratives, the very way innocent stories are told in order to excite interest, gives them a tendency to mislead, then how much scope is there for guilty stories that involve the deliberate use of devices? It would, for example, have been easy to have left out the last section of the narrative, thus giving a slanted picture of an immediate and desperate danger needing to be staved off.

Bad good television

If newspaper stories are held together by sequence, television is held together by contrast. Attempts to maintain balance, and the idea that good television consists of a row between two people who strongly disagree mean that a discussion about the riskiness of a product often consists of a wrangle between some convinced crank with a new cry of doom and the defenders of some established product, who are suitably cautious lest he or she really has got new, if dubious, evidence.

A good example concerns the televisual claim that we are all being poisoned by the mercury in the amalgam of the fillings in our teeth. Not surprisingly, the claim is unfounded[10] but it made a good story for the British television programme, *Panorama*. All of the British population, except for those whose teeth are perfect thanks to fluoride, and an underclass of total denture wearers, have fillings in their jaws. Predictably, then, the claim that that ancient poison mercury could migrate trans-skull, and curdle people's brains caused widespread concern. The leaders of the dental profession who behaved with great dignity on the programme, were made to look foolish because they could not immediately refute the details of this particular attack.

The defenders of a product are always at a disadvantage. By definition they can never prove that a product is safe. They can only reiterate that there is no compelling evidence that it is unduly harmful. The crusader can bring against them what appear to be 'new facts' with all the passion of a zealot, leaving them looking self-interested and out of date. Yet it does not work the other way round. There is little air-time for the innovator who wants a ban removed on the grounds that there is nothing to fear. To say that we were too cautious and too controlling in the past is not news.

Television is also a great confuser, since by its very nature it presents serious matters as part of a sandwich. An important story about the high suicide rate among farmers due to the stress of an increase in regulations can be preceded by a quiz programme, interrupted by an advertising jingle, and succeeded by karaoke. Everything is part of a bizarre and meaningless sequence, quite unlike the solidities of print. The serious is robbed of its seriousness as we entertain ourselves to death.[11]

The rise of the disaster joke
One index of this development is the rise of the disaster joke. There has always been sick humour in the past but the rise of the disaster riddle-joke is a post-television phenomenon.[12] It is a product of a world in which we are shown shocking pictures with a commentary that pretends that seeing the television pictures is equivalent to being present on the spot, when in reality the viewers are sitting safely in their own homes, perhaps eating TV dinners in the midst of famine. We are not living in a global village, but in a global schizophrenia ward. Hence the fast-circulating disaster jokes of the last three decades:

What does NASA stand for?
Need another seven astronauts.

What is worse than glass in baby-food?
Astronauts in tuna.

Cut your risk of getting cancer.
Quit smoking – cranberries.[13]

How do you get an Ethiopian into a telephone box?
Throw a can of baked beans in.
How do you get him out again?
Run past with a tin-opener.

Bemused cow to neighbour: "What do you think about this mad cow disease?"
Second cow: "I don't know. I'm a rabbit."

You need BSE like you need a hole in the head.

How do you catch Salmonella Rushdie?
From curried eggs.

What does a policeman say at closing time in a pub in Armenia?
Come on you lot, haven't you got homes to go to?

Jumbling up the serious and the trivial

When confronted with these jokes, which are one of the few guaranteed genuine products of popular culture, media pundits are apt either to declare that their inventors and circulators (numbered in millions) are evil-minded people with no powers of sympathy or that, by analogy with the morbid humour of those in dangerous occupations,[14] it enables the jokers to cope with the shock of what they are being told and shown.

Both explanations are rubbish. The jokers are normal and numerous and they are not directly experiencing whatever happens to be on the screen, which anyway can easily be switched off. You could not in reality get rid of a famine by changing channels but you can on television. It is this inevitable ambiguity that has given rise to the new breed of jokes.

The very existence of disaster humour, by drawing our attention to the nature of the strange fuzzy mixture of messages that emerges from the television set, also shows why it is so easy to set off a panic, to create a scare or to perpetrate a device on the basis of very little evidence. The paradoxical way in which messages arrive through sandwiches of images means that there is no way of sorting out a serious danger from an ordinary hazard. Even if people are told that a waning tree or a sick leaf may be the product of rapid forest growth and natural selection,[15] the fact that someone is pointing a camera at it implies that there is something wrong and probably that we, the polluters, are to be blamed for it. Yes, it is indeed the time of the acid rains. It would be more rational to ask:

What do you call a leaky car battery outside your house?
Acid drain.

It may seem that acid drain is just a foolish pun, yet it is in fact a likely side-effect of over-reliance on wind-power for electricity. Unless it is supplemented from other sources, the electricity has to be stored on windy days for use in a windless doldrum. This may well involve the use of lead-acid batteries which have been known to leak. Under adverse conditions, living in a wind-powered house could be rather like serving on a World War II U-boat.

An odd jumble of images like the above is exactly what television provides and anyone relying on it exclusively for information and analysis is bound to end up muddled as to what is important and thus to be vulnerable both to authoritarian over-regulation and to alarmist agitation.

Nature: green in tooth and claw

One of the strange factors that enables agitators against a product to employ their devices is the widespread and irrational prejudice in favour of nature and that which is natural.[16] Additives, preservatives, pesticides, weedicides, artificial sweeteners, the irradiation of food, genetically-modified organisms, nuclear power and silicone breast implants are all attacked for being artificial and unnatural precisely because this prejudice exists. Conversely, rival products exploit this feeling by declaring that they are 'safe and natural', 'gentle', 'nature's way', 'free of additives', 'pure' etc. In consequence, we grossly over-estimate the dangers to human beings of artificial, manufactured substances and under-estimate the dangers of nature.

It is difficult, for example, to get people to take sufficiently seriously the dangers of radon, a naturally-occurring radioactive gas that lurks in the cellars of those who live in granite country. Granite is natural and the ancestors have lived here for hundreds of years, so how can it be dangerous? It is difficult to convince the potential victims that the particles and the waves to which they are exposed are the same as in the radiation carefully enclosed within the reactor of a nuclear power station by shielding devices. Likewise the idea that the molecules in a substance from a natural living source may be identical to or very similar to those in a manufactured product is often unacceptable. A kind of nineteenth-century vitalism survives beneath the surface and no amount of demonstrating that a molecule is a molecule is a molecule has any effect on those who believe in it. Chemicals regularly get banned but no-one considered banning vegetables until genetic modifications became possible.

A vivid illustration of this point can be seen by looking at the causes of cancer cited in American news stories whose rank order is almost the opposite of what actually occurs in the real world out there. First then the press reports.

TABLE THREE: Cancer Causes cited in News Stories (1972-92)[17]

Cause	Affirmed	Suspected	Total
Man-made chemicals	304	194	498
Tobacco	236	94	330
Food additives	165	108	273
Hormones as drugs	115	153	268
Pollution	127	95	222
Man-made radiation	124	132	256
Pesticides	117	77	194
Asbestos	104	59	163
Man-made food contaminants	70	69	139
Dietary choices	67	69	136
Sunlight	92	42	134
Other drugs	70	59	129
Natural chemicals	52	32	84
Natural food contaminants	55	27	82
Alcohol	40	39	79
Radon	29	15	44

The only one the American journalists got right was tobacco, probably because of its big business image which overrides the fact that it is an ancient plant originally cultivated by eco-friendly, wisdom-filled Red Indians, whose hoarse coughing voices reveal the secrets of the universe to spiritualist mediums. From then on it was prejudice all the way, with man-made chemicals scoring well above tobacco *even though* pesticides, pollution and other synthetic chemicals are separately listed. This is absurd given that tobacco probably causes up to a third of all cancers.[19] All the artificial potential causes of cancer have been over-reported and exaggerated and appear in the top half of the table. By contrast all the natural causes of cancer such as diet, sunlight, natural chemicals, alcohol and that symbol of the killing stealth of nature, good old radioactive radon, are down at the bottom. For the ignorant American scribblers such factors could not possibly be to blame – they are natural, all too natural. The absurd and misleading nature of this tendency unjustly to blame human activity for cancer and foolishly to exonerate nature can be seen by contrasting the above relative frequencies with which potential carcinogens become the subject of media scare stories with a summary of the estimates of the risks of cancer attributable to different classes of external agent provided by the British scientists Richard Doll and R Peto for the United States Congress Office of Technology Assessment.[20]

TABLE FOUR

Suspected Cancer-causing Factors	Best Estimate of % Caused	Range of Acceptable Estimates
Tobacco	30%	25 to 40%
Alcohol	3%	2 to 4%
Diet	5%	10 to 70%
Food additives	Under 1%	−5% to −2%
Reproductive and sexual behaviour	7%	1 to 13%
Occupation	4%	2 to 8%
Pollution	2%	Under 1 to 5%
Industrial products	Under 1%	Under1 to 2%
Medicines and medical procedures	1%	0.5 to 3%
Geophysical factors (eg sunlight)	3%	2 to 4%
Infection?	?10%	1 to ?%
Unknown	?	?

Easily the largest estimates relate to the effect of tobacco and the diet and these authors comment that they know of no figures to support the common belief that most cancers could be prevented by controlling chemical pollution of the air, food and water or occupational exposure.'[21] Diet means what it says – the balance of natural foods that a person chooses to eat: fat, fibre, sugars, vitamins, minerals etc.[22] The synthetic chemicals added to food may well protect people from cancer due to the beneficial effects of anti-oxidants and other preservatives.[23] By contrast very many foods contain natural substances which if synthesised or extracted as a possible food additive would be banned. We apply double standards to natural and synthetic substances such that much higher (though in absolute terms, small) levels of 'natural' risk are permitted. Eating one raw mushroom which contains hydrazines (a natural pesticide produced by the mushroom itself – mushrooms wish to avoid being eaten) carries with it an estimated risk of cancer that is 1.7 times that of drinking 12 ounces of a diet soft drink sweetened with saccharin.[24] However, no-one tries to ban mushrooms, whereas the Canadian government, who are particularly asinine in such matters, did prohibit the use of saccharin in soft drinks. Saccharin had been extensively used in North America, Britain and Europe for 80 years with no evidence of its causing any harm, but the equivalent of 800 diet sodas a day had proved carcinogenic for Canadian rats.[25] No-one ever subsequently bothered to check the possible level of increased mortality in obesely fat Canadians or in Canadian diabetics caused by their sudden state-enforced switch to natural sweeteners.[26]

Nature's own chemicals much more dangerous than additives

Nature's chemicals exceed in weight and potency as carcinogens those produced by industry by a factor of 10,000 to 1.[27] Synthetic substances are after all less than 0.01 per cent of our daily diet.[28] Food additives are potentially beneficial and the tiny traces of other chemicals such as pesticide residues contain only trivial quantities of potential carcinogens. It is not surprising then that the growth of a modern industrial and chemical-based society has seen a marked drop in the death rate from stomach cancer, and cancer of the oesophagus, the large intestine and the rectum, the very parts of the body that would be most adversely affected if the ingestion of new synthetic chemicals with our food were a major problem.[29] Rather we should ask why cancer of these parts of the digestive system was so much more serious a problem in the bad old days of natural food. The theory that natural foods are harmless because we have eaten them for thousands of years and have therefore either learned to select out the dangerous ones or become adapted to them by natural selection is absurd. Our ancestors knew of the existence of rapid acting poisons in food such as the oxalic acid in rhubarb leaves, but they neither lived long enough nor had they the requisite degree of scientific insight to recognise the possibility of the effects of indulgence in a particular food on their health 30 or 40 years later. Natural selection works only through the relative survival rate of one's offspring and is influenced by diseases that kill children, or kill young adults who thus fail to have children or who by their own deaths leave their children destitute and likely to die. It is unaffected by the diseases of later life; an ability to survive long into old age because of a resistance to some carcinogen or natural long-term poison found in natural foods is irrelevant to the workings of natural selection. It is quite misleading to describe human beings as hardy survivors inured to the natural poisons in their natural foods. Besides, many of these natural foods are new as major elements in our diet; they date only from the beginnings of agriculture in the neolithic era or in any particular part of the world from the growth of international trade.

Nature is man's deadly enemy

How could our ancestors have possibly known which foods were potential carcinogens when they lacked our modern technique of force-feeding rodents with enormous concentrated doses of chemicals to see if they develop cancer or even non-malign tumours? Rodent carcinogens exist in most fruits and vegetables including apples, bananas, broccoli, brussels sprouts, cabbage, mushrooms and oranges.[30] It would be absurd for us to avoid these appetising and healthy foods because of these findings and criminal for the regulatory-environmental complex to legislate against them, but that is no testimony to the wisdom of our ignorant and scurvy-ridden ancestors. Rather it is a measure of our folly in relying so heavily on this mode of testing the safety of synthetic substances in our food and panicking when a new chemical fails to pass a test which would not be passed by many of the natural foods we eat. We are far too trusting of nature and far too unwilling to recognise the pain, suffering and deformity caused both by our natural environment and by our own inner nature, shaped as it is by uncertain, defective and spontaneously mutating genes. Nature is man's deadly enemy. However, there is little point in cursing a non-existent Gaia. Rather we should realise that our own manufactured products are by comparison not dangerous, and refute the attacks made upon them. There can be no place for a double standard in which the risks of the natural are discounted and the risks of the things we invent and make grossly exaggerated. Why should we allow silicone implants, asbestos insulation, saccharine, electric power lines, nuclear power stations or genetically-modified soya beans to be the subject of foolish and unjust attacks by protesters, litigators and regulators when nature is far more threatening?

Irrational patterns of blame

Persons wishing to parade their multi-culturism and relativism have been known to argue that a savage in a primitive tribal society may well have a better notion of cause and effect than a person of a modern, rational, scientific persuasion because he believes in witchcraft. If, as he is entering his hut, the entrance frame collapses on his head and injures him, then he knows that someone has caused it, and that that person is practising witchcraft against him and has deliberately caused this mishap to occur. It would do no good to point out to him that termites had gradually gnawed through the wood over a period of years and slowly weakened it to the point of collapse. This account would fail to explain the coincidence that it fell down at exactly the time when he was passing beneath. At this point modern man runs out of satisfying alternative accounts, for our rational concepts of chance and coincidence, though valid, do not add anything further to the explanation about cause and effect or moral responsibility.[31] In the modern world we no longer have an answer to the question 'Why did it have to happen to me?' In a secular society it is no longer plausible to invoke malign forces or a karmic inheritance from a previous existence. There is no one to blame for the tragedies of accident, handicap, illness, ageing and death that inevitably afflict people.

The rush to blame, especially where children are concerned

Yet the rush to blame remains, particularly if the person suffering some form of harm is a child[32] in a society where levels of infant and child mortality are very low. In the past when children died in droves from infectious diseases or poor and inadequate food no one would ever have considered starting an agitation about a leukaemia cluster, even if they had known what it was. It is very wrenching to visit a Victorian cemetery and to read the inscriptions on the numerous children's graves, yet there is no sense from the evidence of the time that the parents in their grief, or their neighbours in their indignation, were looking for scapegoats for these tragedies. Death in childhood was normal, even for the wealthy.

Today, by contrast, when children are far less at risk, there is a sense of outrage when a child dies – why should this child have died when all the others have survived? Someone must be to blame, preferably an institution or a vested interest, even one remote from the actual event. It is as if in some strange way people feel that they have a right to a reasonable life-span, a right guaranteed by their society, and if that right is violated, then the moral cosmos is disturbed and will not be at peace again until someone has been found to bear the blame. It is this feeling that lies behind the incessant clamour to know the cause behind disease clusters involving children, particularly when there is a blameworthy target in the vicinity. People want to know, even in the face of statistical evidence that there is nothing to know, and to blame, even when there is no culprit. Since it is no longer morally acceptable to make witchcraft accusations against other individuals in the manner of the sixteenth or seventeenth centuries, the frustrated community seeks refuge in junk science and conspiracy theories. Any minor error, inconsistency or withholding of data by technical experts becomes evidence of culpability or of a cover-up, even if it is irrelevant to the main issue.

The scientists working for the drug company producing the anti-arthritic drug *Opren* were attacked on just these grounds[33] even though the accusers' main claim, that *Opren* was a dangerous cause of jaundice, proved totally unfounded.[34] Here of course the agitational mode of thinking links in with the legal-irrational ethos of a bureaucracy in which any breach of rules and procedures is regarded with severity, even when it bears no relation to outcome. Again we see the preoccupation with process rather than product.

The search for someone to blame

The search for someone to blame that leads to irrational attacks on the pharmaceutical or agrochemicals industries and on other products is one that permeates western society. Even our negative moods or emotional states have to be blamed on someone else, as can be seen from the recent irruption of false memory syndrome where unhappy adults or adolescents falsely denounce their parents for having sexually abused them, the 'memory' of this fictitious abuse having been elicited by some cranky psycho-therapist.[35] The same methods (for example, hypnotic regression) can lead people to claim in great and vivid detail that they have been abducted by little green aliens from outer space,[36] or that they are the reincarnation of a medieval monk or an eighteenth-century fish-wife. Since the latter claims are nonsense, it is clear that these methods of eliciting memories of early sexual traumas are hopelessly unreliable, and that their practitioners are probably either fools or frauds. However, these therapists are still in business and are systematically wrecking the lives of innocent families – all because of our culture's obsession with finding someone to blame for each and every individual problem or disorder we face. There is an unwillingness to accept that misfortune may be due to external chance or to the genetic or bio-chemical errors that lurk within us.

Even when there already exists a person who is clearly to blame, as when someone is the victim of a violent attack by a criminal, the notions of blame held in our society are so muddled that immediately we ask irrelevant questions such as 'What "caused" the criminal to do it?' or 'Why didn't someone stop the criminal?' or 'Why were procedures not in place to prevent it happening?'.

Inventing extra people to blame: Dunblane

We can see this scattering of the blame very clearly in the aftermath of the Dunblane tragedy, when a deranged suspected paedophile shot and killed a number of children in a school.[37] The first extension of the blame was quite reasonably to the Scottish police, who had foolishly permitted the murderer to hold a licence to own firearms, even though he was known to be a very peculiar character. Their reason for giving him the certificate seems to have been that he would have made a public protest if it were refused. Then the senior police officials in the organisation would have been embarrassed and would have demanded explanations to make sure that the decision was in keeping with some set of uniform bureaucratic procedures designed to make sure that this particular oddball was not being denied a gun, when other oddballs in Argyll or Caithness were being indulged. The officials making the decision did not wish to be criticised or blamed, even though the blame would not have significantly damaged them, morally, or materially. Like all regulatory bureaucrats they were trapped in a world where the driving concern is to avoid embarrassing those higher up the hierarchy, who in turn are concerned to avoid a political row.

What is ironic about this case is that playing it safe in one sense (to avoid criticism) meant playing it very unsafe in another and it led to the death of the children. Normally, playing it safe leads to excessive caution over health and safety, particularly in the United States, where the bureaucrats' fear of being blamed far outweighs any inner-directed sense of trying to do what is right.

However, the matter did not rest there. The post-Dunblane critics were not satisfied with locating a bad decision nor were they able to see that that decision was made because of the very nature of the regulatory bureaucracies they so much favoured. Predictably, they demanded and obtained more of the same, namely a major tightening up of gun-control legislation. Bad regulation thus led to more regulation, much to the distress of Britain's numerous law-abiding gun-owners. It is yet another case of blame being pinned on a product, against the weight of the evidence, in a way that not only diminishes individual liberty but cuts into the livelihood of small arms manufacturers, gunsmiths, gunshops and gunclubs. Once again a product became a victim of a device. The device was the familiar one of 'defence of the innocent'.

It is interesting to note here that the earlier tightening up of the gun laws in Canada had no significant effect on the Canadian murder rate (though, in fairness, it did reduce the suicide rate among young males).[38] It can safely be predicted then, that there will be no diminution of shootings in Britain either. The entire exercise of blaming a product for a crime is not only unjust to the producers and the willing consumers of the product, but it diverts people's attention away from the evil qualities of violent crime and criminals. To seek to be tough on the 'causes' of crime is not only vacuous but it undermines and contradicts any policy of being tough on crime.

Food additives and crime: failure to acknowledge moral wickedness as the real cause of crime

One of the authors heard it being seriously argued at a meeting held in the Home Office that a key cause of crime was food additives and that disorders in our gaols could be prevented by changing the present prison diet away from criminogenic junk food, and supplanting it with healthy raw vegetables, rice-cakes and herb tea. When the author pointed out that the opposite policy of fattening convicts up had worked very well in preventing escapes from Alcatraz, this was considered to be in bad taste. At lunch all adjourned to the Home Office canteen and everyone except the author produced bottles full of zinc, selenium, iron, vitamins and sundry other pills from their pockets and handbags to fortify their meals. They were all true believers, and as such they could not see the obvious point that crime is not caused by food but is the chosen activity of the morally wicked. Our diets have improved greatly since 1900, but crime has rocketed precisely because we have ceased to pin moral responsibility on individuals and hold them accountable for their actions.[39] The suggestion that food additives 'cause' delinquency in and of itself encourages delinquency, for it undermines the concept of the responsible individual. It provides one more set of neutralising techniques that delinquents can use to disguise from themselves the moral wickedness of their own actions: 'I'm not wicked, I am merely exploited by the food industry.' In this way our muddled ideas about blame which we use to blame harmless products and to exonerate wicked individual criminals contribute to the growth of the real problems of society.

Faced with an enormous growth in crime to the point where it had become a serious detriment to the quality of life of those living in delinquent areas or bad estates, the Home Office reacted by denying that crime had risen as much as people thought, and asserting that the real problem was not crime but the fear of crime. By implication this could best be reduced by persuading the potential victims to be less timorous. That they thought they could get away with this argument is a measure of the peculiar double standards that operate in our society. One can imagine what would happen if the public relations department of a major industry were to declare 'Pollution levels have not gone up ten-fold, they have merely tripled' or 'It is not pollution but the fear of pollution that is the real problem'. What we can see from this is that the issues have been distorted so that we are perpetually engaged in blame-wars disguised as disputes about empirical evidence. The aim of those who have gone to war is to divert society's capacity for blame away from wicked individuals committing crimes, fathering children they won't support, and descending into addiction, and to pin it instead on those who produce what the others steal. Those who support such an ideology are in a very real sense enemies of the people.

What whistle-blowers gain from their activity

The subscribers to this ideology use a whole range of myths to try and blame and discredit not only the producers but also their scientific experts, as happened in the case of *Opren* discussed earlier. *Opren* has been exonerated but this has not prevented critics from demanding that the task of providing and processing scientific information for the regulatory agencies should be taken away from the pharmaceutical industry itself and given to some independent quango.[40] The usual device of using slogans such as 'detachment', 'impersonal impartiality', 'proper procedures' has been employed to justify a yet greater degree of bureaucratisation in society, which would in this case lead to a slowing down of the rate of pharmaceutical innovation and to no discernible improvement in drug safety.[41] It is also a gross libel on the impartial and well-intentioned scientists who work in industry.

The ideological antithesis of the 'villainous' in-house scientist is the heroic whistle-blower who is held to be devoid of self-interest and incapable of dishonesty. Yet whistle-blowers do have something to gain from their whistling and it can lead them into scientific fraud themselves. Also, the fraud, if undetected, is irreversible, for, in safety testing, ordinary scientific replication may not be required before a result is taken seriously and used as the basis for implementing a ban. If biased scientists in the pharmaceutical industry were to fudge their results to cover up dangerous findings, it would do them little good because some other group of scientists would repeat their tests and discover that the drug was dangerous, and then it would be banned anyway. By contrast, if a whistle-blower produces fraudulent evidence that a drug is harmful and is not found out, the failure of other scientists to reproduce these findings may have little effect. The one negative result may be enough to damn a product.

Whistle-blowers who cheat are thus in a position to do a lot of damage as one can see from the strange tale of Willie McBride. Dr William McBride, an Australian obstetrician, was, in 1961, one of the first persons to observe that women given the drug thalidomide during pregnancy produced children with severe abnormalities. It was an observation that brought him fame, recognition, prizes and a research institute called Foundation 41. He was the very prototype of the heroic whistle-blowers who attack a remote and irresponsible industry to prevent human tragedy. Yet in 1988 an independent enquiry held that he had committed serious scientific fraud.[42] He was utterly discredited.

Being on the politically correct side more important than telling the truth

McBride had fed the drug hyoscine (scopalamine) to pregnant rabbits to see if their litters were deformed. However, in writing up the experiments he altered his data, and when the number of rabbits with observed abnormalities proved too few to be significant, he added two more rabbits, later claiming that the extra rabbits had been sent to Virginia for dissection.[43] When questioned about inconsistencies in relation to the quantity of the drug consumed by the rabbits in their drinking water, he asked rhetorically 'What is more important, a child's life or how much a rabbit drank in an experiment?'[44]

We can see here the very epitome of the false idea that motive determines truth. McBride was claiming that because he was on the side of the children and against the big pharmaceutical companies, he could not have been guilty of fraud,[45] even though he obviously was, and was found guilty. Yet without detached, accurate, objective sets of observations of how much a rabbit drank, it was impossible even to begin to protect children, since the knowledge of how to do so would be unavailable. Later the same year, McBride defended himself in the same terms saying 'the committee said if only one rabbit produced deformed foetuses the results would not be significant. That's cold comfort to the mother of a malformed child.'[46] Again he was exploiting a false antithesis between our emotional response to tragedy, particularly a tragedy of innocence involving mother and child, and the need for accurate measurement and diagnosis.

Debendox and *Imipramine*

It is this type of argument, rather than the chemical relationships[47] between the drugs *per se*, that seems to link McBride's experiments on hyoscine to his campaign against the drug *Debendox*. *Debendox* was used to treat morning sickness during pregnancy. McBride claimed, on the basis of somewhat flimsy evidence, that it caused deformities. In the United States the parents of children with deformities sued the manufacturer and McBride gave evidence for them. Nothing was proven against Debendox but the company was forced to withdraw the drug because of the cost of the litigation.[48] Another product had become a victim, and the pregnant women who had been taking it had either to switch to a less satisfactory and possibly less safe drug, or to endure severe nausea, which can bring with it dangers of its own. We are worse off without *Debendox*.

Prior to this, McBride made a number of attacks on other drugs taken by women in pregnancy, notably the tri-cyclic anti-depressant imipramine in the early 1970s. McBride's arguments were not accepted by the Australian Drug Evaluation Committee. Nonetheless on 6 March 1972 the Director-General of Health sent telegrams to doctors, urging them not to prescribe imipramine to women of child-bearing age in case they unknowingly became pregnant.[49] The Australian tabloid press accepted what McBride said, not because he had any evidence but because of who he was. There was a full-scale techno-moral panic with pompous headlines such as, 'Something is very seriously wrong with a system which so clearly fails to protect the public against the dangers of modern drugs.'[50]

The main victims of all this were pregnant women taking anti-depressants. If, as a result of the panic, women had suddenly come off the anti-depressants, plunged into an emotional abyss and committed suicide, then their deaths, or the damage done to foetuses by failed suicide attempts, would have been just as much the result and the fault of those starting the panic as birth deformities were the result of thalidomide. Whistle-blowing carries risks but they are rarely measured.

What we do know is that many pregnant women in Australia and elsewhere responded to the panic by having abortions.[51] In 1973 McBride declared, 'I personally feel that if a woman needs anti-depressants she shouldn't be pregnant and is better off having an abortion. If you can't cope with life before a child arrives you'll be much worse off afterwards.'[52] Doctor knows best. Others may well wish to ask, who was to blame for this quite unnecessary destruction of human life and the emotional distress of the seriously depressed women scared into abortion in this way?

It is difficult to know McBride's motives because he still refuses to admit that there was any wrong-doing.[53] However, the suspicion must be that he was a whistle-blower.[54] Whistle-blowing brings fame, excitement, glamour and a sense of inner-righteousness that are every bit as tempting as material rewards. Also if you do commit scientific fraud, as McBride did, you are likely to get away with it. McBride was only questioned because his junior research workers claimed he had changed his figures and went public; whistle-blowers have their own whistle-blowers. Also even if his work had never been replicated by others, the one set of (fraudulent) experiments by McBride might still have been enough to cast a blight, not only on the substance he used in his experiments, but on other related drugs. It is not a question of science, but of regulation and litigation, especially in the United States where lawyers circle in the court room thermals.

We have to emancipate ourselves from the crude myths of our society that divide the world into corporate villains to be blamed and heroic whistle-blowers and eco-warriors who can do no wrong. We must go beyond goodies and baddies. Indeed in matters of health and safety and the environment it is doubtful whether the moral rhetoric of guilt and innocence, praise and blame is at all appropriate.[55] Rather we need an *ethic of consequences* that is concerned not with the ideological probity of the actors in a situation but with the consequences of their actions.

4

Where we are at

The regulators and the regulated: monopoly and danger
Due to the massive rise not in risk but in regulations in western societies in the last half of the twentieth century, we have become regulated societies in which there are two identifiable 'classes', the regulators and the regulated. The units of the regulated vary in size from the large corporation to the lone individual but none of them have the crushing monopoly power of a national agency of state like the American FDA (Food and Drugs Administration), or of an international treaty or agreement (such as the ban on CFCs), or of the interlocking cogs of regulations that constitute the EC and the CAP. Try buying vitamin B6 or Bombay duck nowadays.[1] Faced with German obduracy over genetically-modified organisms or the foolishness of the FDA over silicone implants, the greatest of private corporations is helpless and unable to defy the regulatory-bureaucratic complex. Many health-safety-and-environment activists may well applaud this situation because ideologically they are anti-individual choice, anti-capitalist and in favour of an enhanced state.

Regulated societies are unhealthy and polluted: Russia and China
Conveniently, they forget that the worst pollution in recent history occurred in the socialist countries of Eastern Europe.[2] Air pollution in the former East Germany, Poland and Czechoslovakia damaged both the lungs of the people and the trees of the region on a scale not to be found in the West, except in border areas exposed to

socialist pollution when the wind changed direction.[3] Matters were even worse in the Soviet Union, the only industrial country in the world where longevity was declining due to the impact of pollution from heavy industry on living conditions.[4] It is likely that a similar disaster will soon overtake China. Worst of all, contrary to a strict international agreement, signed by the USSR, secret KGB factories at Dzerzhinsk and other sites poured large quantities of PCBs (polychlorinated biphenyls) into the river Nemen that flows into the Baltic Sea. It could in time have killed off all life in the oceans.[5]

The Eastern disasters were all the product of a fiercely guarded state monopoly of political and economic power. There was a regulating class in socialist Eastern Europe, one that regulated society in the interests of building up its own power and expanding heavy industry regardless of the impact this had on the environment or the health and safety of the people. It was a truly despicable kind of society. However, the key problem was not just that the people in power in Eastern Europe were badly motivated but that potential dissenting groups in the society such as the medical profession, scientists or journalists were not allowed to provide sufficient organised criticism of their rulers. A dispersion of political power is the key to a balanced policy. *Any* kind of monopoly regulator is bound to make mistakes, whatever its intentions.

Corporations are weak and divided; regulators enjoy monopoly power

Contrary to what is often suggested by agitating activists, those who are regulated do *not* form a cohesive, let alone monolithic, group. On many health or environmental issues business corporations are divided among themelves on the grounds of self-interest alone. If a particular product is forced off the market then its nearest competitor or subsititute benefits. What is bad regulatory news for saccharin is good news for the makers of other artificial sweeteners, and what is bad news for artificial sweeteners in general is good news for sugar, and vice versa. Likewise, if alcohol is in trouble, it is good for soft drinks. The world of business is far weaker and more fragmented than that of the regulators, and companies will even do research to suggest that a rival product is unsafe. There is disagreement and conflict everywhere and many companies take a green line because it is good for their particular business. The manufacturers of expensive high-quality binoculars and telescopes are strong environmentalists because of their high level of sales to bird-watching twitchers, and the British house insurance industry is locked in combat with the producers of hydrocarbons over the possibility of global warming. The insurers are fearful lest climatic instability lead to bigger insurance claims for damage caused by storms or subsidence. The regulated, then, cannot easily defeat their regulators by forming an all-powerful coalition. What is far more worrying is that one section of the regulated class can always ally itself with the regulators to put weaker rivals out of business. Sometimes the bigger units are aggressive and push for 'higher' standards of health and safety that they know their smaller rivals can't meet, even though there is no need for them and the 'reforms' will also push up their own costs. The bankruptcy of their rival and the resulting growth in market share and monopoly power more than compensates for one's own higher costs. Consumers lose out because prices go up, choice is reduced and a monopoly has been established; but then consumers are an untidy nuisance who insist on deciding for themselves in matters that the regulators feel are much better left to regulators.

Big business can accommodate regulations, small business goes under: the case of slaughterhouses

A more common scenario is that the bigger producers simply passively accept any new regulations proposed by the regulators, and the regulators proclaim that they have achieved a consensus. Small protesting losers who cannot bear the cost of the new regulations are ignored and treated as backward, unhygienic and irrelevant, regardless of whether the new regulations were necessary in the first place. The cost of a regulation is often a fixed cost regardless of the volume of production and so falls hardest on the smallest producers. Many small abattoirs which used to be run by owners who were also small farmers or butchers, for instance, have gone out of business because they cannot afford on their low turnover the scale of veterinary fees (which is the same regardless of how many pigs are killed per day) demanded by the new regulations introduced over the last decade.[6] As old slaughterhouses close down, the remaining slaughterhouses are now situated further apart and animals have to be transported longer distances before they can be slaughtered, which in turn has led to more regulations and less animal welfare. It's a funny thing about regulations; the more of them you have, the more you find you need.

The main consequence of the EU's hygiene directives has been to increase the consumer's chances of food poisoning due to the flourishing of harmful organisms in meat from animals transported long distances to the slaughterhouse under stressful and overcrowded conditions.[7] Once again, more safety regulations mean less safety.

Advertising bans are a form of protectionism

Regulations also favour established businesses over new entrants. It might be supposed for instance that the French alcohol and tobacco industries would be opposed to the new French regulations, which restrict the advertising of alcohol and tobacco in France. On the contrary they are pleased and may well have helped to bring the new regulations about. The French producers' main fear is of the penetration of the French market by foreign products, such as Scotch whisky replacing brandy, wine from Chile or California competing with French wine, increased sales of foreign cigarettes and so on. These new foreign entrants can only prosper if French consumers are made aware of their availability through advertising. This is, of course, advertising's main purpose; indeed it is why the advertiser is a heroic figure, a champion of freedom who provides discovery in an age of restrictive regulation. Thus, the best way for the French manufacturers to prevent damaging competition from foreigners is to prevent advertising, which will, of course, freeze and preserve their present market shares. The French healthists are triumphant because they have won a major symbolic victory, and become part of a long and authoritarian French tradition. The French manufacturers are pleased because they have closed and protected their market. The only losers are the consumers, whose choices have as usual been curtailed. But what French government ever cared about freedom of choice?

The costs of regulation to clients

The same point can be made in relation to the drive by the Lord Chancellor, with the assistance of the big law firms, to compel solicitors to be franchised (ie, to accept state regulation and direction) before they can defend criminals on legal aid. In addition, in future, the franchised solicitors will only be able to brief certain selected counsel and call expert witnesses who have been approved by the state. In effect, this will mean the death of the law as an independent, free profession and defence lawyers will become part of a state-controlled bureaucracy.

Many have objected to this change on the grounds that, at present, clients can choose who represents them, and clients often prefer an independent firm. The franchisers have replied that clients do not know what is in their best interest, ie, that they, the regulators, know best. They have, of course, produced no evidence that this is the case, and they have made no proper comparison between the efficacy, from the *client's* point of view, of matched samples of franchised and, thus far, unfranchised firms. Rather it is asserted *a priori* that the franchised firm gives the better service because it meets certain irrelevant formal bureaucratic criteria laid down by the regulator. In the future a criminal client may well be forced to abandon the solicitor who has served him (in all senses) honestly during a long criminal career and to submit to being defended by a bureaucratically-approved stranger. We have no reason to suppose that the client's health and safety, ie, freedom from mistaken conviction,[8] from unreasonable refusal of bail or from inappropriate sentence will be in any way enhanced by this growth in state-franchised regulation at the expense of individual choice. The clients will probably be worse off because they will be forced to go to large firms for whom criminal legal aid work is a small and neglected part of their overall interests, or to factory firms whose staff turnover is high and whose geographical coverage is so broad as to exclude the kind of local knowledge necessary for the job.

It seems very likely in many of these cases that the client would have fared *better* if the regulations and regulatory agency had never existed in the first place. Even if this were not the case we might still be a better society if we had fewer regulations and individuals were free to make mistakes and to reap the harmful as well as the beneficial consequences of their choices. The moral superiority of our society over those of the former socialist societies of Eastern Europe lies not so much in our cleaner air and rivers as in the ability of our citizens to make a wider range of choices. Even if the old socialist states had gone for health and ecology instead of heavy industry and weapons, they would still have created a servile society where someone else made your choices for you. Those who believe otherwise secretly hope that in a cowardly new world of more regulations they will be the regulators and all will be well. The rest of us ask *Quis custodiet ipsos custodes?* Who is to guard *The Guardian* readers?

More costs and consequences of regulation
However, both regulators and agitators demanding more regulations tend to disregard questions about the growth of state power and the diminishment of individual freedom of choice, and to argue the case for regulation in terms of its beneficial consequences. In effect they argue that citizens are better off because they have been protected from things that are noxious or dangerous. Up to a point it is a reasonable argument, but it is not necessarily a justification of the particular level or degree of regulation to be found in any of the specific modern industrial countries such as Britain, Canada, the EC Eurostaat, Germany

or the United States that we have discussed in our case histories. Also, even if many of the regulations and prohibitions are justified, it does not follow that this is true of any particular regulation enforced by the regulators or advocated by the agitators. Indeed, in the case histories cited earlier, we have shown many cases of products under attack either by regulators or by agitators where there was no such justification.

The attackers tend to take the view that their errors are mere errors in the direction of yet more safety, which therefore don't matter. 'After all', they say, 'You can't be too careful, can you?' Oh, yes you can. Additional restrictions can be harmful both in their own right and because they increase the already over-large volume of regulations with which we are forced to comply. However, most of the costs and consequences of excessive health, safety and environmental regulation never get mentioned, let alone measured. In our case histories we have already pointed out the considerable problems caused by regulation and regulation-agitation in particular cases; here we will outline the general problems that arise from a failure to be sceptical where regulation is concerned.

Particular persons and statistical persons

Those who seek to justify a particular prohibition commonly point to particular deaths, or damage to particular persons, that could have been avoided if a prohibition had been in force at the time. This was what was (falsely) alleged for example by the agitators who drove the drug *Opren* off the market.[9] It is a potent argument, especially when applied to the past, though it should be noted that the tighter health and safety regulations become, the less validity this kind of argument has. It might well have been valid to argue in the 1860s or the 1950s for tighter health and safety regulations. It does not follow that it is reasonable to do so now. Each extra increment of regulation on top of all those that already exist is, other things being equal, going to produce a smaller improvement in health and safety, to the point in many cases where it is close to zero, or even has a negative effect. At the same time it may well be that the increased cost and aggravation caused by that same extra increment of regulation may well be greater than for any comparable clutch of regulations introduced in the past. Regulation is a form of taxation. Britain already has a universal system of VAT, from which no-one is exempt. It is called regulation. Regulation is theft.

The costs and nuisances associated with increased regulation get neglected because they do not just fall on certain particular persons, but on all of us; and we are seen as mere statistical persons.[10] If Fred Smiggs dies after taking a particular drug prescribed by his doctor, and the coroner comments adversely about it, it is quite possible that there will be an agitation calling for the drug to be banned. Fred Smiggs is a particular person with whom we can all identify. In consequence the government may ban the drug, or tighten up the regulations generally. Each of these responses carries with it indirect costs that are often neglected. The first of such costs falls on those who were previously also taking the drug who may be forced to switch to another less suitable drug, such that they die younger than they would have done on the old drug, are cured more slowly, or suffer severe new side-effects. These problems may be noted by observers, but only in relation to the other remedies, and not as a consequence of the loss to patients of the original drug eternally associated with the deceased Smiggs. These indirect victims of the ban are at best mere statistical persons who exist only as numbers, unlike Mr Smiggs who became known to all when he died, by courtesy of the coroner, the press, the agitators and the politicians who were determined that 'Smiggs shall not die in vain'.

Such groups commonly ignore the fact that their actions may have caused more harm than they prevented. Skilled and sophisticated regulators, insulated from immediate political pressures might, it is true, be able and willing to take into account the factors we have cited and to redress the balance between particular persons and statistical persons in favour of the latter. However, in a democracy the Smiggs factor is always present and any local disaster is likely to result in a burp of new regulations from the politicians. Also there are other categories of statistical persons who appear even more remote, the number of whose members is difficult to measure and whose interests are hardly considered at all. The hidden price of Smiggs-type legislation is that not only the production costs but also the development costs of new products rise enormously.

Regulations push up the cost of pharmaceuticals and deny patients remedies

It costs on average about £160 million to take a new drug from conception to the market-place, vastly more than was the case in the past, and a significant part of this increase is a result of the need to comply with stricter regulations. In consequence many potentially life-saving and harm-relieving drugs never become available at all, and others are delayed for years.[11] The average development time now is about 12 years[12] and a decade of patients dies or suffers without them. These are the invisible statistical victims of over-regulation whose interests rarely get taken into account.

The problem could be avoided by patenting and marketing drugs in third countries, rather in the way that shipping companies register their vessels in Liberia or Panama to avoid regulations, but drug companies dare not risk their reputations in this way. In consequence drug manufacturers have to be large multi-nationals since the cost of meeting regulations makes it difficult for small companies to survive or to enter the market.[13] Attacks on products have had many other kinds of harmful indirect consequences. Perhaps the worst of these is the one we term 'the alternative iron cage'.

The alternative iron cage

The price that has to be paid for living in a healthy, wealthy, low-risk, advanced industrial society is that our lives are controlled and constrained by an iron-cage[14] of our own and other people's calculations that demand of us perpetual diligence, con-scientiousness, self-control and perseverance. We cannot go hunting, fishing, rearing BSE-ridden cattle, or critically criticising, just when we feel like it in the manner idealised by Karl Marx and Freidrich Engels[15] because we are all trapped in a network of contracts, duties, responsibilities and obligations. It is the price we pay for living three score years and ten – not as a maximum life-span but as an average expectation – for having a regular and sufficient supply of food, for having escaped the idiocy of rural life so extolled by greenists, for having a variety of analgesics, contraceptives and medicines and for having abundant supplies of energy available at the flick of a switch; none of these were to be had in the pre-industrial world. Whether we have gained or lost overall by entering the iron cage is a matter of individual preference but in any case it is too late to go back, so we have to learn to live with and within our bars.

However, the latter part of the twentieth century has seen the growth of an additional iron cage, that we have termed the 'alternative iron cage', a new cage that constrains the individual within legal and extra-legal shackles, purportedly imposed for the benefit of health, safety and the environment. It is as if each of us were trapped in two cages simultaneously with one cage tilted at an angle of 45 degrees to the other, leaving very little room for its harassed occupant:[16] the trap of work and the trap of safety. Also it is very often difficult to discern the purpose of the bars on the new alternative iron cage. It is one thing to be prevented from hunting as and when we choose, due to pressure of work and lack of money, as postulated by Karl Marx; it is far worse to be told that we may no longer hunt foxes or stags and are obliged to shoot only the hapless politically incorrect ruddy-duck because particular small urban elites have, largely from irrational spite and prejudice, enacted new rules with which to constrain us.[17] The growth of the alternative iron cage has meant more regulations, more bureaucracy and more surveillance for everyone, ie, a lower quality of life, supposedly in the interests of health, safety and the environment. No one knows where the oxen are going but the goads and pricks point in all directions and are a torment to all.

Let the reader ask him or herself the following questions: 'How much information have I recently been forced to provide for some external agency or an internal monitoring stooge?' 'How much did it cost me or my colleagues in terms of resources, stress and nuisance?' and 'How much did *they* pay for the information they took away with them?' 'A great deal' will be the answer to the first two questions, and 'nothing' will be the answer to the second? Precisely. Regulators, including those involved in the bogus search for those modern snarks turned boojums known as 'Quality', 'Standards' and 'Excellence', all believe that information is a free good. They do not pay for it and they do not care what the collection of the data costs those who are being regulated. Often the data is useless, and collecting it has no purpose other than to placate the regulators and to demonstrate their arbitrary power. In turn the regulators are often unable to make use of the excessive weight of data delivered unto them. They are unable to process it, and they often simply can't understand it. This would be a wonderful farce but for the horrendous effect it has on people's working lives – the fear that the snoopers will come, the frantic preparations for their inspection, wherein 'procedures' and 'paper trails' are invented and back-dated to deal with all possible breaches of the regulations; the retrospective invention or re-writing of tauromerdine solutions to problems that arose in the past, but have now been resolved.

Very real threats to health and safety are often successfully concealed, for example by hiding illegal and unsafe electric heaters and kettles in filing cabinets, and illusory threats are magnified in order to show how health and safety conscious the staff are. Worst of all, a thicket of defensive bureaucracy is created whose purpose is not to prevent accidents or damage or failure but to deflect away blame should something go wrong. The offending department, secure with its paper trail of lies, knows in advance that in the event of a disaster it can safely bleat that 'all the proper procedures were in place and were followed to the letter'. The existence of highly developed levels of defensive bureaucracy is a mark of a sick organisation with a defective organisational culture and bad leadership; however, the real villains are those who orchestrated the external pressures that led to this dysfunctional and defensive response. If you constrain individuals and groups within unrealistic rules, and goad them with unattainable demands, then they will cheat in order to survive and succeed.[18]

More regulations mean less truth respected

Ironically the most recent case of such scientific improvisation has been falsely blamed on Glaxo-Wellcome, the respected pharmaceutical firm. In seeking to promote one of its products, Glaxo-Wellcome had distributed to doctors copies of research reports from professional scientific and medical journals showing that the product was safer than, and superior to, its rivals. It was subsequently shown that these publications were not independent of one another, but that some of them consisted to an extent of research surveys that incorporated other researchers' previous findings. So much for peer-review as a guarantee of quality. Thus the *nth* article favouring the Glaxo-Wellcome product might have been little more than a word-processor scissors-and-paste job on the previous ones, together with a few new pieces of data, ie, it was not really new and independent evidence in favour of the company's product.

Glaxo-Wellcome, however, were in no way to blame for the irruption of this kind of pseudo-publication. Rather it was the institutions who employed the scientists or which provided them with grants who were at fault. By imposing fake bureaucratic measures of 'productivity' on the scientists, they made it much more likely that scientists would improvise using a mixture of plagiarism, salami publishing and lack of innovation. It is indeed ironic that the misdeeds of the total quality control bureaucratic complex should have been detected by their health, safety and environment rivals, though quite deplorable that Glaxo-Wellcome should have been made to carry the can for it.

These bureaucratic grids are part of an alternative iron cage of regulation, surveillance and propaganda that damages the quality of people's working lives. No one disputes that we need some rules relating to health, safety and the environment, but these are now so extensive that at the margin they may well be costing more lives than they save due to the increased stress, occupational uncertainty and alienation experienced by those forced to live and work in an excessively bureaucratic world. Attacks on products whether from regulators or from agitators only exacerbate the problem. We are all the victims of excessive and pointless regulation and surveillance by one agency or another and we must fight it, not just when it impinges on us directly but, and as a matter of principle, in defence of others.

What is not to be done

A demand for rapid de-regulation might well prove as disastrous as the present process of hyper-regulation, since it is difficult to know where it is safe to start dismantling, though a beginning could be made by unravelling the legislation that made possible some of the attacks against particular products discussed in our section of case histories. In addition all regulations emanating from the EC should be far more slowly and erratically administered by the United Kingdom than they are at present in order to achieve full harmonisation with Southern Europe. Let us apply EC rules with the speed of that asthmatic carapaced reptile, Britain's traditional Fabius tortoise. Let us rebuff the insolence of office with the law's delay. However there are four rather more general social points that need to be made in relation to everything that has been discussed, namely that we need: selective openness; more scepticism; the use of markets in place of regulations where appropriate; and a permanent campaign against irresponsible ecohealth agitators.

Selective openness

In many respects it is tempting to advocate for Britain the kind of openness achieved by the US Freedom of Information Act in order to expose the arbitrary, blinkered and authoritarian nature of, say, the Home Office, or the Lord Chancellor's Department, which routinely, and for dubious reasons, refuse access to their files – even if the files are now in the Public Record Office and of interest only to historians, or were freely open for inspection in the past, but have now been retrospectively closed for 'policy' reasons. The excuse given is that the individuals mentioned in the files might object. (On the contrary they want their grievances made public.) The real reason is that these government departments wish to conceal the foolish errors and occasional wrong-doing of civil servants, lawyers and police officers. They do not wish the public to know just how incompetent their regulators are; it would 'undermine public confidence'. Yes and quite right too. Why should we be expected to have faith in a secretive and defective system of government?

However, it is more difficult to make the same kind of criticism of many of the British regulatory bodies dealing with health, safety and welfare, except where they are administering some absurd Eurodiktat. In surveying our case histories we have been struck by the fact that the most absurd cases of pointless and destructive bureaucratic over-regulation are drawn from countries other than Britain, notably Canada, Germany and the United States. The reason for this seems to lie in the traditionally collegial[19] and collaborative nature of British institutions, a tradition now sadly being eroded as the bureaucrats take over. The regulation of the pharmaceuticals and chemical industries, for example, is carried out by officials who are professionally qualified in the same field as those whom they monitor, who usually work on a close and friendly basis with them and who routinely have access to firms' most highly confidential data on a voluntary basis. In other words, the regulators are trusted; they are not just faceless bureaucrats but known persons of good character, rather like local as opposed to national inspectors of schools. If there is a problem, you can tell the local inspector, knowing that this will not result in a malicious prosecution for a trivial reason such as slightly and briefly exceeding emission limits (the equivalent of being done for speeding at 32 mph). Between them the industries and the inspectorates of the environmental agencies have achieved a high level of success in integrated pollution control based on the pragmatic principle of BATNEEC – Best Available Technique

Not Entailing Excessive Costs.[20]

However, this system is now under criticism from agitators who see it as too cosy and insufficiently transparent, even though it is easy enough for them or anyone else independently to measure any gross or growing air and water pollution, and to do the appropriate chemical tests. Indeed, some companies have been known to analyse the waste discharges of their rivals in order to learn what they are producing and by what method, especially if it is thought to be a new process. This is the main reason why chemical firms do not wish to state publicly and in detail the nature of each and every chemical that has been wrongly released into the environment. It would destroy commercial confidentiality, which is why firms' reports about discharges into the environment tend to be couched in generic terms such as 'an alcohol', 'an aldehyde' etc. The inspector knows the full details but there is little point in publishing this highly technical information which only specialists can understand and which would be misused by half-educated activists, as we saw in the attack on Shell over Brent Spar; there would be more unjustified scares and panics, with all the extra cost and nuisance involved. Worse still it would mean the prising apart of the inspectors and the inspected who presently have a co-operative relationship and the creation of a mistrustful, antagonistic, legalistic, bureaucratic system which would not only be less effective but would create a very unpleasant working environment for everyone – another alternative iron cage.

The problem with whistle-blowers
One of the odder responses to a recent spate of accidents on the railways and elsewhere has been the suggestion that there should be a whistle-blower's charter, a guaranteed immunity for anyone who reveals a breach of health, safety and environmental regulations by the institution that employs them or to which they belong.[21] On matters such as the exposure of unsafe signalling practices on the railways or slipshod safety checks on ferries, there is clearly a good case to be made for protecting from reprisals the whistle-blower who saves lives or could have saved lives if he or

she had been disobedient. An operative who refuses to work or to let pass an unsafe machine or system and reports the fault to outsiders is a hero. However, most cases are not of this heroic kind. In all walks of life people routinely break minor health, safety and environmental regulations without any deadly consequences. They have learned by experience that some prohibited risks are trivial and so they take minor risks in order to avoid the effort, cost and tedium that living by the letter of the legislation would demand. If every petty risk-informer and ecograss were to be cosseted for drawing this to the attention of the authorities, many enterprises would grind to a halt. Organisational survival is only possible because many bureaucratic rules are broken much of the time.[22]

In any case, why should this kind of whistle-blower be given special protection, when libertarian whistle-blowers, who seek to expose the foolishness and oppressiveness of a regulatory agency in order to curb its powers and curtail its reach, are not so protected? In the course of our work we spoke to many lawyers, dentists and teachers who had been lucidly and intelligently critical of those who constrained and regulated their professions, and attacked their 'product' in the name of those three great lies, 'quality', 'standards' and 'excellence'. Yet none of them was willing to be quoted by name for fear of reprisals, for fear that the regulator might, in retaliation, deliberately spend a disproportionate amount of time going over their work or doing over their institution in search of minor errors from which a malicious case against them might be constructed. In the case of the employed professionals, their main fear was that even if their description of a particular act of folly by an inspecting agency were suitably anonymised by us, it would still be recognised by their immediate superior, or by the head of their institution, who would be plunged into a lather of terror lest the inspectors find out; these fearful little gaffers would then abuse and bully all possible whistle-blowers for the sake of retaliation and deterrence. These critics of the system ought also to be protected by any future Public Interest Disclosure Bill.[23] It is just as important that the inept operations of, say, legal franchising, which may result in the innocent, impoverished reader ending up in jail following a mistaken conviction[24] be exposed, as it is to report the breach of a health or safety regulation that might possibly result in injury.

A call for general scepticism

Studies of this kind often end with a plea for more regulations, more research or more education. Such pleas usually correspond closely with the self-interest of the authors. We make no such detailed requests, as we neither possess the dogmatic certainty of such writers about the nature of the evidence, nor their confidence in the need for regulation; nor do we feel that more research and education of the kind already purveyed in large quantities would do very much good. The farce of the 'educational' campaign against a non-existent heterosexual epidemic of AIDS,[25] the wrangles over dietary guidelines,[26] and the teaching of environmental 'science' in schools instead of physics and chemistry, do not inspire us with confidence. In an ideal world everyone would study some basic scientific methodology, elementary statistics, and the analysis of fallacies and of the use of misleading devices of language. In practice, if such instruction were introduced it would only get pushed into an already overcrowded and badly thought-out school or college curriculum taught by overworked and bureaucratically harassed teachers, and would achieve nothing. Politics is the art of the impossible and knowing not to attempt it. Likewise, selectively to fund research into possible though unlikely risks is to distort the allocation of funding. It encourages scientists to mislead at the level of getting grants (even if their final results are honest), since the best way of getting funded is to talk the risk up. Even when it is clear from the initial results that it is unlikely that any serious risk exists, the possibility of a new risk-orientated gravy-train influences the researchers to conjure up further dangerous possibilities and uncertainties that have to be investigated.

Rather, we have only one piece of advice to offer: 'be sceptical'. The public are already sceptical in one direction, namely concerning statements on risk issues made by industry, and by certain branches of government such as the Ministry of Agriculture, Fisheries and Food.[27] The disastrous handling of the BSE/CJD crisis was enough to ensure that. Levels of mistrust are even greater in countries such as the United States or Germany where there is a long tradition of a 'paranoid style' in their politics, and an unhealthy obsession with creating a world of material and metaphorical purity, cleanliness and perfection.[28]

However, it is not this kind of mistrust that we are asking for. What we seek is a quiet, stoical, balanced scepticism in which ecohealthist agitators are equally seen as people who should not be believed; it is time to do without trust and certainty, for in the low-risk modern world they are not really needed. It is not that the agitators are malign, though some of them are, but merely that they are claiming a degree of certainty that is not humanly possible. Anyone who uses agitprop language, as we can see from our earlier case histories of the attacks on Shell and Nestlé, is bound to be wrong. We live in a world where there is much less risk than in the past, but risk can never be eliminated entirely. We must calmly accept that there can be no certainties, and that all human activities carry with them some degree of risk, however small. The healthists and greenists, whom we have criticised in detail for their fatuous and reckless attacks on blameless companies and products, are absurd, utopian crusaders who deserve to be ridiculed and the falsity of their propaganda systematically exposed. At present they do not receive their fair share of scepticism and disbelief because they are seen as idealists, and not primarily motivated by material gain. History should have taught us that idealists who head or staff movements directed towards goals elevated above our normal quotidian concerns have always proved the biggest liars. Consider the historical record of our very own British communists who, not for financial reward but from an attachment to an ideology, spent their entire lives mendaciously defending vile dictatorships that had murdered tens of millions of people. Now that old reds have given way to new greens why should we be any less sceptical of people with this kind of utopian and ideological mind set?

Britain's regulators are in general a far more balanced and better informed array of people than are the agitators; indeed we have singled them out for praise in comparison with many of their counterparts in Germany and the United States. Nonetheless they too should be regarded with scepticism. Every time there is a crisis or acute disagreement over some aspect of health, safety, the environment, the law or education, a committee is set up full of supposedly eminent persons, one of whom is chairman and gets the report named after him or her and possibly also a title or trinket from the government for services rendered. For the next decade this necessarily fallible document is treated as if it were divine revelation and constrains subsequent policy. Yet all such documents are, of necessity, a patched-up agreement between a group of worthy but fallible human beings; we may be forced to accept a committee's findings because it has the powerful backing of a democratic government, but we still ought to regard such reports with great scepticism. There is a very good chance they got it badly wrong. The non-existent heterosexual AIDS epidemic again comes to mind.

Be sceptical about scientists
Whilst the British people have learned by experience that lawyers and educationalists make disastrous policy mistakes, and have come to despise those responsible for such errors for their arrogance and foolishness, there still exists in some circles the illusion that science is objective, precise, accurate and reliable. Yet science, like the government committees that pronounce on policy or, indeed, like all human interaction, is a social construct.[29] The question of whether a particular experimental result is valid or whether a particular hypothesis has been confirmed is decided by means of agreements between groups of scientists acting within their relevant institutions. Every so often it is decided that yesterday's science, which was thought to be true at the time, is false and must be discarded. Science is provisional and falsifiable: that is its strength.[30]

We would not wish to push the social construction of science argument too far as it can lead to the absurd view that we cannot say that there has been progress in modern science, on the grounds that it cannot be proven with absolute certainty that, say, our knowledge of chemistry today is any better than it was in 1950 or 1900. Whilst it cannot be proven with utter certainty that this is the case – in theory, chemists could discover in 2050 that they had regressed since 1950 by pursuing false ideas – it is extremely probable that there has been considerable and irreversible progress, since nearly all the evidence points in that direction and we do not have to rely on the beliefs of the chemists to demonstrate that is the case. By contrast, it is very debatable whether the philosophy, sociology, literary criticism, political theory, educational 'thought' or theology of today are any better than those of some decades ago; there are many who would say that one or more of them has got worse or been subject to absurd changes of fashion.[31] However, the traditional physical sciences are – at least in the long-run – reasonably immune from this kind of criticism, not completely so, but very largely so. We can be sure beyond reasonable doubt, as they say in criminal trials, that there is progress in science, something that cannot be said of any other human activity. We cannot be absolutely certain of this but it is pointless to demand such certainty. Certainty is not to be had in the affairs of ordinary mortals.

No consensus on meat
Nonetheless when scientists sit on regulatory and advisory bodies of necessity they become part of them and cannot and should not appeal to the long-term achievements of their discipline to boost their own authority. They are dealing in this context with recent and contestable data that can be interpreted in many ways, and their work involves them in making value judgements and subjective estimates of probability. The 'scientific' conclusions of such government bodies should accordingly be treated with a great deal of scepticism. Ultimately an official committee's views are merely the views of one reasonably well-qualified group of people.

They could well be wrong. The fact that science and health policy are mere social constructs is well brought out in a report by the science editor of *The Times*[32] about disagreements within the government's advisory committee COMA:

Fresh doubts have been cast on government advice that eating red meat can increase the risk of cancer.

The committee responsible has yet to agree on the final wording of its report, even though the recommendations have been published in a press release from the Department of Health on September 25.

The Department last night denied that any changes were planned in the wording of the key advice on red meat, but there are known to be disagreements within the Committee on the Medical Aspects of food policy (COMA) over how strong it should be.

The original version, written by a panel headed by Professor Alan Jackson of Southampton University, favoured warning only those who eat 140 grams or more of meat a day. This advice was incorporated into the report and sent to the printer. But at the last moment two members of the full committee demanded stronger language.

One of them was Professor Philip James, director of the Rowett Research Institute in Aberdeen, the nutrition expert responsible for producing a report at Tony Blair's request on how the new Food Standards Agency should be organised. After Professor James objected, copies of the report were scrapped and a new version prepared incorporating stronger advice. This said that anybody eating the current average intake of red meat or above (90 grams per day) "should consider a reduction".

The revised version was discussed at a COMA meeting on October 21. Professor Jackson, with the backing of his panel, is understood to have expressed reservations about the new wording.

He indicated that the advice his panel had originally drafted was as much as the scientific evidence justified. The result is a stalemate, with no date for the final publication of the report and no clarity over what government advice on meat really is... The latest muddle will infuriate ministers who have already been embarrassed by the need to halt the printing of the first version.

No doubt all the parties concerned acted in good faith, and we have no wish to tread on COMA toes. Indeed it is unfair of their critics to accuse them of muddle or for failing to provide clear government advice. Honest muddle in the face of uncertainty is better than a pretence of omniscience.

The need for periodic reconsideration and repeal of regulations

Even when 'clear advice' is offered by the government on the eating of red meat it should be taken with a pinch of salt. Any such advice should be regarded with scepticism as it is based on probability calculations that are of necessity uncertain and on statistics subject to alternative explanations. That is how it always is. Yet once an agreement on clear advice *has* been achieved by COMA as a result of political pressure, it will be peddled by health educators as if it were of guaranteed *ex cathedra* infallibility, and the honest doubts of the dissenters will disappear down a black hole in history. Another reason for scepticism, and enjoying one's meat.

One reason we fail to be sceptical about the regulators is that we rarely consider the penalties and the failures of their success. Whenever there is a techno-moral panic, new regulations and new restrictions are introduced but they are rarely ever reconsidered later, let alone repealed. Because 10 years on, people are still relieved to have escaped what had been thought to be an impending disaster, they are unwilling (a) to look backwards and ask whether they might well have been safe anyway and avoided the cost and nuisance of the regulations; (b) to look sideways at other countries that took no action and suffered little or no adverse consequences. The studies of Wildavsky and others have demonstrated time and again that this is the case,[33] but our institutions are quite unresponsive because we live in an unreflexive society. We are always peering forward at tomorrow's possible dangers and yet it is only by considering the ways in which we foolishly over-reacted to illusory techno-moral panics in the past that we can know how to respond to them rationally. An 'alarmed' outer perimeter fence around a secure institution that is set off by cats, sparrows, hailstones and supposed UFOs wastes the guards' time and resources and in the end allows the enemy to sneak through. We must look backwards, and respond with scepticism.

An ecohealthist is a person who knows the value of everything and the price of nothing. In consequence he or she has no sense of proportion and no capacity for judgement. Ecohealthists are apt to mouth slogans such as 'we have got to put health and safety first' while being unable to see that this is a value statement and not a statement of fact. It may well be that we should give a high priority to health and safety much of the time, but there are occasions when it would be immoral to put them first. Those who work themselves to death and gain an important objective by their sacrifice may be heroes rather than fools, and the same may be said generally of men and women who pursue risky occupations or who fight dangerously for liberty against a totalitarian state. There are always other competing values that human beings can and sometimes should prefer.

Life is not of infinite value
A similar foolish healthist slogan says that 'human life is of infinite value', a statement that is meaningless within our finite human world. Indeed this loose use of the word infinite is the exact counterpart of the healthists' use of the word zero when they demand that the safety of a product should be proven and that there should be zero risk. They do not live in the real world or rather they slide between the real world and the land of rhetoric and metaphor so fast that they do not know where they are. In practice we do not and cannot treat human life as of infinite value

103

because there are other competing human values, even in a field such as road safety, and where road accidents are one of the biggest causes of death for young people.[34] In principle a very large reduction in the number of both fatal and non-fatal accidents could be achieved by preventing young males aged 17 to 25 from driving motor vehicles. At present the only restriction on them once they have a full licence consists of the high insurance premiums they have to pay because of the horrendous number of accidents young, male drivers cause. If they were banned from our roads, many lives would be saved. However, we do not take such drastic measures, partly because we know they would still drive illegally and without insurance and possibly with forged documents, partly because of the economic costs incurred if this age-group were unable to drive (even in the army) and partly because it would be an interference with these young men's *rights*. Driving is so central to our society that to deprive an adult whose own personal driving record is immaculate of the right to drive merely because he belongs to a particular age-sex category would be wrong and discriminatory.

At a more silly level, there can be a clash between nationalism and road safety as when the Welsh language brigade insisted that all road signs in Wales be bilingual, ie, in Welsh as well as English. It would come as no surprise to us if we were to learn that a number of drivers have crashed while trying to decipher an ugly squiggle of meaningless consonants saying *Gwynt o'r ochr* or *Arafwch nawr* or even *Croeso i Loegr*. [35]Yet, by the time the *gwynt* has hit from the *ochr*, it has ceased to be *nawr* and it is too late to *arafwch*. Clearly, placating the conceit of the tiny Welsh-reading minority among the sons of Gomer is more important than notching up a small safety improvement.

Language wars in road safety
A more impressive case comes from Belgium, that crumbling, dysfunctional microcosm of the European Community, which like Wales is plagued by an absurd language war, as can be seen from

Petersen's description of the shaping of road safety policy in that country:[36]

> A law was proposed to set a speed limit of 90 kilometres (per hour) on ordinary two-lane roads retaining the prior absence of any limitations only on the major four-lane highways with limited access and other safety features. But one Walloon member of parliament pointed out that most of these better roads are in Flanders whose inhabitants would thus enjoy the right to drive faster than French-speaking motorists. Some of the older roads in Wallonia were, therefore, exempted from the speed limit in order to extend the privilege over an equal distance in both sections of the country even though this would presumably mean a higher death toll among Walloon drivers and their families.

We are not in any way sympathetic to the bigoted linguistic chauvinism of Gwalia or Wallonia but we accept that people can and will decide not to put safety first when other issues are at stake. Health, safety and ecology may be utterly central for activists, but for most people they have to compete with other goals and values – with wealth, pleasure, amusement, achievement, knowledge, asceticism etc. Individuals have different trade-offs between these entities and it is impossible to know anything about these except by observing and reacting to the signals given by prices in the market place. However, most regulators (except perhaps those working closely and collaboratively with industry) are not in the market place and can have no idea what any particular regulation is worth. Any system of shadow prices or pseudo markets used to get round this problem is of questionable value since the relationships are arbitrary and can be altered at will by the powerful, as in the legendary French cost of living index which contained an inordinate number of ping-pong balls. Official index numbers, or the placing of things in rank order, are not an objective measure of success or failure: they merely reflect one group of people's arbitrary and subjective preferences. Under these circumstances it may not be worth expending a large amount of resources in gathering expensive new data about any one factor or dimension of the situation, since it would have to be balanced against other items that can only be estimated and in a manner that is essentially and necessarily problematic. Indeed increased precision may be dangerous and misleading if it causes people to place a quite unjustified faith in one particular variable, formula or approach. We must be sceptical. The world is always more complicated than it is made out to be.

A market in risks

It might be easier for most people if there were more of a market in health and safety. Let the state continue to provide basic protection, particularly in areas where the risk is a collective one, but otherwise leave people to make their own choices. Competing, licensed, private agencies and testers could then offer certificates of 'extra-safe' or 'extra-healthy' to products passing their tests, which would then enjoy a premium price determined by the degree to which the purchasers valued extra increments of health and safety, and the costs of extra insurance. In such a world it would be possible to bring drugs on to the market that have not been subjected to all the increased testing imposed during the last 30 years when standards of safety have been irrationally high. Had the present drug regime been in place when they were discovered, drugs such as aspirin (internal bleeding), paracetamol (liver damage) or penicillin (individual allergic reaction) would never have been made available to the consumer but banned as unsafe.[37] Why should their modern 'unsafe' equivalents of similar value to the consumer not be marketed with a compulsory label saying they have passed various safety tests but not all of them. It is then up to the consumers to assess the risks for themselves, much as they do in the case of playing rugby league, going skiing, riding a motor-bike or drinking the many carcinogens present in a cup of coffee.

Products would, of course, need to be labelled more carefully than they are now to alert individuals to their riskier contents, which, though not detrimental to most people, could be harmful to particular susceptible (for example allergic) individuals. This would necessarily mean an increase in proper quality packaging in order to hold the extra warning labels. Manufacturers would also need to be strongly discouraged from adding irrelevant information about, say, irradiation, genetic modification or the country of origin of a product, which would act as 'noise' drowning out data vital to the health of particular individuals, though perhaps this too would also be best left to the market. Let the customer decide.

5

How companies can fight back against regulators and agitators

In our studies of attacks on products we have been surprised at how difficult it has been for even major industries or large firms to resist their attackers, whether regulators, or agitators, without sustaining substantial material or political loss. A scattering of trouble-making pressure groups can inflict immense damage through malicious libels (against which there is no real redress, since the damage is done and the liars are paupers), through acts and threats of vandalism and terrorism, through rent-a-crowd protests and through mass-media-supported boycotts. The politicians who alone control the use of legitimate force are never willing to take strong enough action against greenist illegalities and often give legitimacy to the protesters by negotiating and conceding. It is an amazing demonstration of how, in capitalist societies, economic power does not command political power. Politicians want growth and taxes but they are unwilling to back those who produce them against those whose mission is to attack and destroy products and thus the very wealth of society on which we all depend. What can producers do to protect themselves? We have four suggestion.

First, companies (and indeed professions) must shift their entire public relations effort from one of crisis management to one of crisis prevention. They must be prepared to fight the activists on a continuous basis by obtaining detailed intelligence about agitators who are potentially hostile to their operations, cultivating a network of media contacts and ensuring a steady flow of accurate stories detrimental to their opponents and undermining their credibility. If necessary this should be done in an indirect and unattributable way. Do not wait for an attack, but strike first; discredit the opposition now, in advance, using the same media tactics that they employ, but with the advantage of having better and more honest information than they do.

Secondly, be ready instantly to mobilise those whose political and economic interests depend on the continued prosperity of a company or industry: its workers, suppliers and distributors, and the local authorities and the local media in the main areas of production, together with any major institutional shareholders. They are all important sources of public opinion, political influence and economic pressure. Also they can be used to boycott the boycotters. If the healthists and greenists try to hit sales revenue they should be reminded that advertising revenue can also be employed to exercise pressure.

Thirdly, competing companies should agree to compensate one another in cases where one of their number is affected by an irrational greenist-healthist agitation that could equally easily have fallen on any one of them. Thus in the case of the violence and the threatened boycotts of Shell over the Brent Spar issue, the other oil companies out of self-interest as well as moral duty, should have offered to compensate Shell for any losses incurred in defying the agitator, whether from arson or from consumers switching to other kinds of petrol.

Finally, industry and the professions must learn the importance and force of ideology and the need to win ideological as well as market-place battles. It is myopic merely to respond to a particular political climate, to adjust and to trim, and to see the brief changes of the last five or ten years as inevitable, irreversible and bound to continue. Anyone who doubts this should read the nonsense that academics were writing in the 1940s about the inevitability of nationalisation, in the 1960s about the need for indicative planning and price controls, or in the 1970s about the triumph of trade union power. It was all nonsense and it did not happen. It is always possible to change the inevitable. In the light of this it is clearly foolish to be supine in the face of enhanced regulatory power or the coercive tactics of single interest pressure groups. Industries and professions should do their *own* long-term social and political research – not mere opinion polling – and not rely exclusively on other institutions for their information and ideas. Much of what the latter provide is mere ideology – often anti-producer ideology – wrapped in a legitimizing methodology. Overall objectivity can only be achieved if competing studies are done from within a competing ideological framework – one favourable to the producer. Such an ideology should not be based on the crude promotion of economic prosperity, valuable though it is, but be explicitly libertarian in character. It is better for Britain to be free than risk-free. We need an ideology that brings home to all both the restrictive and limiting qualities of the alternative iron-cage and the chaos caused by the agitators. It must be made clear that when products are attacked we are all under attack.

Biographical notes

Dr Mark Neal is Lecturer in Industrial Sociology at the University of Reading. He is currently researching into the hidden costs of health, safety and environmental regulations, particularly those concerning the pharmaceutical, chemical, food and biotechnology industries. In 1995 he wrote *Keeping Cures From Patients: The Perverse Effects of Pharmaceutical Regulations,* London, Social Affairs Unit. Dr Neal has further research interests in comparative and international management; he has a PhD in International Management and is the author of *The Culture Factor: Cross-Cultural Management and the Foreign Venture,* Macmillan Business. He has also carried out extensive research on the gambling industry. He teaches Organisational and Industrial Sociology at Reading University, and also a Masters course in Risk and Regulation.

Professor Christie Davies is Professor of Sociology at the University of Reading where he teaches the sociology of morality and a master's course unit on Death and the State. He has been a visiting lecturer in India, Poland and the United States and has taught in Australia. He holds a first degree in Economics and a PhD in Social and Political Sciences from the University of Cambridge. Professor Davies is the author of books on criminology, the sociology of morality, censorship and humour and his work has been published as book chapters or in journals in Australia, Bulgaria, Canada, France, Germany, Greece, Hungary, India, Israel, Italy, Japan, Poland, Switzerland and the United States as well as the United Kingdom.

Notes and references

Chapter 1

1 By the term 'techno-moral panic' we mean any widespread and disproportionate public panic about the effects of an artificial process or product upon health, safety or the environment.

2 See Philip E Ross, 'Lies, damned lies and medical statistics', *Forbes Magazine*, 14 August 1995, pp 130-135; JR Johnstone and C Ulyatt, *Health Scare: The Misuse of Science in Public Health Policy*, Critical Issues No. 14 Perth: Perth Australian Institute for Public Policy 1991; Stephen Milloy, *Science Without Sense: The Risky Business of Political Health Research*, Washington: CATO Institute 1995.

3 The use of shocking images by campaign groups include: the famous little mouse with the human ear growing from its back (anti-genetic engineering); any number of foxes being torn to shreds (anti-hunting); the surgical scars used in a propaganda campaign by the vegetarian society and condemned by the Advertising Standards Authority (meat being 'carcinogenic' leads to operations and therefore scars); a close-up photograph of Leah Betts, the girl who died after taking ecstasy (anti-drug); and, of course, the use of tombstones in the awareness campaigns about the non-existent heterosexual AIDS epidemic.

4 See Henry Miller, *Biotechnology Regulation: the unacceptable costs of excessive caution,* London: SAU, 1997.

5 See Marcia Angell, *Science on Trial - the clash of medical evidence and the law in the breast implant case,* London: Norton, 1996.

6 Nestlé, *Nestlé and Baby Milk,* Croydon: Nestlé, 1994.

7 Reiner Luyken, 'Die Protest-Maschine', *Die Zeit,* 37, 9, 6 September, 1996.

8 Mark Mills, 'Reactions to Health and Environmental Risks', Peter Berger et al, *Health, Lifestyle and Environment: Countering the Panic.* London: SAU, 1991, pp. 104-110.

9 Mills, op cit.

10 Bernard Davis and Donald L Ritter, 'How Genetic Engineering Got A Bad Name', *Imprimis,* 18(2) February, 1989, pp. 1-5; Malcolm Gladwell, 'Risk Regulation and Biotechnology' *The American Spectator,* 22 (1) January, 1989, pp. 21-24.

11 For a useful discussion of this issue, see Miller, 1997, op cit.

12 Ibid, p 13.

13 Ibid, p 9.

14 Florianne Koechlin, *Which variety of species do we need?* Munchenstein: Munchenstein European Co-ordination, 1993.
15 Miller, op cit.
16 Ibid, pp. 9-10.
17 For a fascinating discussion about the contemporary obsession with 'naturalness' see Anthony O' Hear. *NonSense About Nature,* Risk Controversies 9, London: SAU, 1997. Also, see Frank Furedi, *Culture of Fear: Risk Taking and the Morality of Low Expectation,* London: Cassell, 1997, pp. 27-28.
18 This is an issue that is largely ignored by pressure groups who demand ever-increasing consumer information. It is our view that legal requirements for information on packaging should be strictly restricted to proven health risks. For a typical call for over-labelling see The Pure Food Campaign, 'Risks of genetically engineered foods', *Third World Resurgence,* No. 38, 1994, pp. 18-19.
19 There is of course a 'politics' of ritual pollution and what is acceptable to one group of orthodox Jews may not be acceptable to another; there is a corresponding 'politics' of food labelling.
20 John E Mack, *Abductions: Human encounters with aliens,* New York: Charles Scribners and Sons, 1994.
21 Miller, op cit.
22 See Richard Rhodes, *The Making of the Atomic Bomb.* Harmondsworth: Penguin Books, 1986.
23 'Electric Shock - Electromagnetic Fields', *Post Magazine* 15/2/ 96; 'Fields of Doubt - Do Electomagnetic fields damage your health?' *Electrical Review,* 13/5/94, p 28; 'Millions risk cancer from power lines - report'; *Reuter News Service,* United Kingdom 05/10/95; Petr Beckmann, *Electromagnetic Fields and VDT-it is,* Boulder, Colorado: Golem Press, 1991; Richard Sanford, 'Shocking Distortions Versus the Current Truth on Electromagnetic Fields', *S.O.S. Alert* (Society for Objective Science), 2(1), January, 1994, p 1.
24 Mills, op cit.
25 Ibid.
26 Ibid.
27 Eg, 'Leukaemia may be linked to infection, study finds', *Reuter News Service,* United Kingdom, 03/11/94.
28 Chris Baker, 'AWE licensing leads to public anger, anti-nuclear campaigners attack surveys' clean bill of health', *Newbury Weekly News,* 3 July 1997.
29 Ibid, Section 2, p 1.
30 Ibid.
31 Ibid.
32 Jolyon Jenkins, 'The Cluster and the Fluster', *The Guardian,* 17 June 1997.
33 Ibid.
34 Mills, op cit, p. 109.
35 British Medical Association, *Living With Risk: The British Medical Association Guide,* Chichester: John Wiley and Sons, 1987, p. 43.
36 Ibid, pp 130-1.
37 Ibid, p 95.
38 See Aaron Wildavsky, 'If Claims of Harm from Technology are False, Mostly False, or Unproven, What Does That Tell Us About Science?' In Berger et al ,

op cit, pp 111-145.

39 Aaron Wildavsky, 'Wealthier is Healthier'. *Regulation*, 4, 1980, p. 10.

40 See, DB Jeliffe, and EFP Jeliffe, *Human Milk in the Modern World*, Oxford: Oxford University Press, 1983; WHO, *Women and Breast Feeding*, Geneva: World Health Organisation, 1983.

41 Nestlé, op cit.

42 Ibid.

43 International Baby-Food Action Network, *Breaking the Rules*, London: IBFAN, 1994.

44 Nestlé, op cit.

45 See Aberdeen University Research and Industrial Services, *Removal and disposal of Brent Spar – a safety and environmental assessment of the options*, 1994; Shell, *Brent Spar Abandonment Impact Hypothesis* prepared for Shell UK Exploration and Production by Rudall Blanchard Associates Limited 15/12/94; Shell, *Brent Spar Abandonment - BPEO Assessment* Prepared for Shell UK Exploration and Production by Rudall Blanchard Associates Limited 15/12/94; Smit Engineering BV, *Feasibility Study - Phase I, II and II - Report for Scrapping of the Brent Spar*, 1992, Contract to Shell UK Exploration and Production.

46 Financial Times Energy Economist, 'Brent Spar: A Strange Affair', London: *Financial Times Energy Economist*, July 1995.

47 'Greenpeace loses some of its veneer during double blast', *Wall Street Journal*, 7 September 1995.

48 'Green for Danger', *Daily Telegraph*, 21 June 1995.

49 'Greenpeace Fiasco', *Daily Telegraph*, 7 September 1995.

50 *Wall Street Journal*, op cit.

51 *Greenpeace Annual Review* 1993-4, KPMG Accountants, June 1995.

52 Reiner Luyken, 'Die Protest-Maschine', *Die Zeit*, 37, 9, 6 September 1996; Wolfgang Mantow and Jens Pocleus. *Die Ereignisse um Brent Spar in Deutschland*, Hamburg: Wolfgang Mantow Kommunikations-beratung, 1996.

53 See *Brent Spar Abandonment - BPEO Assessment*, op cit.

54 John Davidson, 'A platform for punchy propaganda', *Sunday Times*, 25 June 1995.

55 Minette Martin, 'Fight the Bad Hype', *Sunday Telegraph*, 11 September 1994.

56 *The Independent*, 22 June, 1995.

57 European Crop Protection Association, *Revision of the Drinking Water Directive and the Uniform Principles - Socio-economic impacts*, Brussels: ECPA. September 10 1993 (C/93/DG/845).

58 Ibid, p 2; see also, Word Health Organisation, *Revision of the WHO Guidlelines for Drinking Water Quality*, Geneva: World Health Organisation, 1992.

59 *Deregulation Now: Report of the Anglo-German Deregulation Group*, Bonn: Federal Ministry of Economics, 1995, p 18.

60 For an excellent discussion of the wider issues raised by the silicone implants controversy, see Marcia Angell, *Science on Trial: the clash of medical evidence and the law in the breast implant case*, London: WW Norton and Company, 1996. For a precis of the story, see Angel, ibid, pp 19-32.

61 Ibid p 19.

62 Council on Scientific Affairs, American Medical Association, 'Silicone Gel

Breast Implants', *Journal of the American Medical Association*, 270, no 21, 1993, pp 2602-6; Angell, ibid, p 21.

63 W Bunch, 'Under the knife: Woman uses razor to remove implants', *Newsday*, April 18, 1992, p 7; Angell, 1996, op cit.

64 Celia Hall, 'USA: Breast Implant Damages Sought by 10,000 women' *The Independent*, 26 November 1994.

65 W Carlsen, 'Jury awards $7.3 million in implant case', *San Francisco Chronicle*, 14 December, 1991, p 13; Angell, op cit.

66 Angell, op cit.

67 Peter Berger 'Towards a religion of health activism', Berger et al, op cit, p 29. Also see Peter Berger, 'Furtive Smokers - and What they tell us about America', *Commentary*, Vol 97, No 6, June 1994.

68 For a good overview of the research see Robert Nilsson, 'Is environmental tobacco smoke a risk factor for lung cancer?', Roger Bate (ed) *What Risk?* Oxford: Butterworth-Heinemann, 1997, pp 96-151.

69 Indeed, we have uncovered a clear tendency for activists and bureaucrats to cite aged studies that back their causes, long after they have been subjected to scientific scrutiny and discredited. Junk science is clearer and more convenient for their purposes than proper science, which often produces ambiguous results that are useless for campaigning purposes.

70 The relevant publications were D Trichopoulos, A Kalandid, L Sparros, and B MacMahon, 'Lung cancer and passive smoking', *International Journal of Cancer*, 27, 1981, pp 1-4; D Trichopoulos, A Kalandid, and L Sparros 'Lung cancer and passive smoking', *Lancet*, Sept 17 1985, pp 677-678; T Hiriyama, 'Non-smoking wives of heavysmokers have a high risk of lung cancer: a study of Japan', *British Medical Journal*, 282, 1981, pp 183-185; T Hiriyama, 'Cancer mortality in non-smoking women with smoking husbands based on a large-scale cohort study in Japan', *Preventative Medicine*. 13, 1984 pp 680-90.

71 Campaigners around the world use the concept of 'causality' as if there were only one factor involved in the development of cancer.

72 See Nilsson, op cit.

73 Environmental Protection Agency, *Respiratory Health Effects of Passive Smoking: Lung Cancer and Other Disorders*, Environmental Protection Agency, 1992.

74 Nilsson, op cit; Kevin Dowd, 'The Myths of Anti-Smoking', *Economic Affairs*, Vol 11, No 4, June 1991; Peter Finch, 'Misleading claims on Smoking and Health'. *Policy*, Vol 6, No 3, Spring 1, 1990; CJ Smith et al, 'Environmental Tobacco Smoke: Current Assessment and Future Directions', *Toxicology Pathology*, Vol 20, no 2, 1992, pp 289-303.

75 See, JR Johnstone and C Ulyatt, *Health Scare: The Misuse of Science in Public Health Policy*, Critical Issues, No 14, Perth: Australian Institute For Policy Study, 1991.

76 Trichopoulos, et al, 1981, op cit; Trichopoulos, et al, 1983, op cit.

77 Hiriyama, 1981, op cit; Hiriyama, 1984, op cit.

78 See, for instance, the initial critique of his results by, N Mantel, 'Non-smoking wives of heavy smokers have a higher risk of lung cancers', *British Medical Journal*, 2, 1981, pp 914-915.

79 For example, America's Environmental Protection Agency.

80 *Environmental Tobacco Smoke and Lung Cancer: An Evaluation of the Risk*, Report of a European Working Group, April 1996; Nilsson, 1997, op cit.
81 *Environmental Tobacco Smoke and Lung Cancer: An Evaluation of the Risk*, op cit., p v.1; Nilsson, op cit.
82 See Nilsson, 1997, op cit.

Chapter 2
1 Details taken from Table I, 'Original Objections to Pasteurization', in Morton Satin, *Food irradiation: a guidebook*, Lancaster, Pa: Technomic, 1993.
2 O'Hear, op cit.
3 See, Mary Douglas and Aaron Wildavsky, *Risk and Culture*, University of California Press, 1982; also see, Aaron Wildavsky, *Searching for Safety*, London: Transaction Books, 1990; and Mary Douglas, *Risk and Blame: Essays in Cultural Theory*, London: Routledge, 1992.
4 We thus disagree with Ulrich Beck's analysis of reflexivity, particularly that espoused in his classic book *Risk Society*. See Ulrich Beck, *Risk Society: Towards a New Modernity*, London: Sage Publications, 1991.
5 See British Medical Association, op cit, p 130.
6 For discussion of the acid rain debate see Dixy Lee Ray, 'The Great Acid Rain Debate', *American Spectator*, 20 (1) January 1987 pp 21-25. Also see Henry C Scuotguaza 'Acid Rain: Neutralising a Myth', *On Principle* III (3) 6 February, 1984, pp 6-7.
7 Aaron Wildavsky, *But is it true? : a citizen's guide to environmental health and safety issues*, London : Harvard University Press, 1995, p 100
8 Ibid.
9 Ibid. See also Emile Durkheim, *Suicide: A Study in Sociology*, London: Routledge, 1989.
10 Sue Kelly, John Charlton and Rachel Jenkins, 'Suicide deaths in England and Wales, 1982-92: The contribution of occupation and geography', *Population Trends*, No 80, Summer, 1995, pp 16-25.
11 Durkheim, op cit.
12 Christie Davies, 'What prevents life from being worthwhile?' *The World and I*, 3, 5 May, 1988, pp 665-85.
13 Wildavsky, 1995, op cit, pp 72-3.
14 Ralph Keeney, 'Mortality Risks Induced by Economic Expenditures', *Risk Analysis* 10, No 1, 1990, pp 147-159.
15 Wildavsky, 1995, op cit, p 272
16 See Mark Neal, *Keeping Cures From Patients: The perverse effects of pharmacuetucal regulations*, London: SAU, 1995.
17 For an interesting discussion of the case of asbestos, see Etienne Fourniew and Marie-Louise Efthymiou, 'Problems with very low dose risk evaluation: the case of asbestos', in Roger Bate (ed), *What Risk?* Oxford: Butterworth-Heinemann, 1997.
18 For a discussion of *Opren* and *Zomax* see David Green, *Medicines in the Marketplace: A Study of Safety Regulation and Price Control in the Supply of Prescription Medicines*, London: IEA Health Unit, 1987.
19 British Medical Association, 1987, op cit, p 130.

Chapter 3
1 Miller, op cit.
2 Christie Davies, 'The great legal aid franchising fraud', *The Lawyer*, 2 December 1997.
3 John C Luik, *Pandora's Box: The Dangers of Politically Corrupted Science for Democratic Public Policy*, Bostonia, University of Boston, 1994.
4 Andrew Gilligan, 'Honey not safe for young children, parents warned', *Sunday Telegraph*, 18 May 1997.
5 Ibid.
6 Ibid.
7 Ibid.
8 Others fail to be alarmed by the ambiguous nature of honey. Who cares whether it is solid or liquid?
9 Gilligan, op cit.
10 Simon Wesley, 'Annoying Dose of Doubts', *The Times*, 14 July, 1994.
11 Kenneth Minogue, *The Silencing of Society, the True Cost of the Lust for News*, London SAU, 1997.
12 Elliott Oring, 'Jokes and the Discourse of Disaster', *Journal of American Folklore*, 100, 1987, pp 276-86.
13 Wildavsky, 1995, op cit, p 11.
14 Jack Haas, 'Learning real feelings: a study of high steel ironworkers' reactions to fear and danger', *Sociology of Work and Occupations*, Vol 4, No 2, May 1977, pp 147-170; Jack Haas, '"Binging", Educational control among high steel iron workers', *American Behavioral Scientist*, Vol 16, 1972, pp 27-34.
15 Wildavsky, 1995, op cit, p 294.
16 O'Hear, op cit.
17 Adapted from S R Lichter and S Rothman, *Scientific Opinion vs Media Coverage of Environmental Cancer*, Washington DC: Centre for Media and Public Affairs, 1993. See also Wildavsky, 1995, op cit, p 380.
18 SR Lichter and S Rothman, 1993, op cit.
19 British Medical Association, op cit.
20 Ibid, p 39. A summary based on R Doll and R Peto, *The Causes of Cancer* London, OUP, 1981.
21 British Medical Association, op cit, p 39.
22 Ibid, p 64.
23 Ibid.
24 Aaron Wildavsky, op cit, p 32.
25 Ibid.
26 At the time of the ban in 1977, there was no other synthetic low calorie alternative. Cyclamates had been banned even earlier.
27 Wildavsky, op cit.
28 Ibid.
29 British Medical Association, op cit, p 37.
30 Wildavsky, op cit.
31 See, for instance, Bryan Wilson, *Magic and the Millenium*, St Albans: Paladin, 1975; E Evans Pritchard, *Witchcraft, Oracles and Magic Among the Azande*, Oxford: Clarendon Press, 1937.

32 'The Rush to Blame', *Daily Telegraph,* 30 March 1994.

33 John Abraham, 'Distributing the benefit of the doubt: Scientists, Regulators and Drug Safety', *Science, Technology and Human Values,* 19, 4, Autumn 1994, pp 493-522; John Abraham, 'Scientific standards and institutional interest: Carcinogenic risk assessment of benoxaprofen in the UK and the US', *Social Studies of Science,* 23, 1993, pp 387-444; John Abraham, 'Negotiation and accomodations in expert medical risk assessment and regulation: An institutional analysis of the benoxaprofen case', *Policy Sciences,* 27, 1994, pp 53-76; John Abraham, 'Bias in Science and Medical Knowledge: The Opren Controversy', *Sociology,* 28, 3, 1994, pp 717-736. In this series of articles John Abraham claimed that the scientific assessment of drug trials was influenced by vested interests that sought to ignore, dismiss or obfuscate unfavourable results. Abraham thus sought to challenge the notion that scientific standards were applied consistently or (for want of a better word) 'objectively' in the testing and monitoring of drugs.

34 See, British Medical Association, op cit, p 129.

35 A further absurdity that can be induced in this manner is the belief that one is the reincarnation of of a long-dead person. It has been known for two separate individuals both claim to be the reincarnation of one and the same ancient Egyptian queen.

36 Mack, op cit.

37 At about the same time, a similar tragedy took place at Port Arthur in Tasmania, and produced a similar knee-jerk response.

38 The suicide rate among young males in Canada had been rising, but it levelled out as it became more difficult for them to commit suicide impulsively using a gun.

39 Christie Davies, 'Das Verbrechen in einer burokratisierten Welt'. *Der Monat,* 293, 1983, pp 47-67.

40 See Note 33 to Chapter 3.

41 See Neal, op cit.

42 'Fraud in Sydney?', *The Lancet,* 12 Nov 1988 II, p 1153; Murray Hogarth, Bernard Lagan and John O'Neill, 'The Foundation and the Fall', *Sydney Morning Herald,* 19 Dec 1988; Norman Swan 'Baron Munchhausen at the lab bench?', in Stephen Lock and Frank Wells (eds), *Fraud and misconduct in medical research,* London, British Medical Journal Publications Group, 1996, pp128-143.

43 Bill Nichol, *McBride, Behind the Myth,* Sydney: ABC, 1987; Norman Swan, Science Show ABC Radio, 12 Dec 1987.

44 Nichol, op cit.

45 William McBride, *Killing the Messenger,* Cremorne, Eldorado, 1994.

46 Nichol, op cit.

47 Ibid, pp 145 and p 233.

48 Ibid, p 142.

49 Ibid, p 39.

50 Ibid, p 40.

51 Ibid, p 40.

52 Ibid, p 44-45.

53 McBride, op cit.
54 Nichol, op cit.
55 Christie Davies, *Permissive Britain,* London: Pitman, 1975.

Chapter 4
1 See, 'Stress drug rule drives health shops into collapse', London: *The Sunday Telegraph,* July 13 1997.
2 Andrezj Werner, 'Marxism and Pollution - Some East European experiences before the revolutions', Schleicher, op cit, pp 291-303; and Stanislaw Uziak 'Soil Pollution and its consequences', in ibid, pp 141-153.
3 Christie Davies, ' Politics Requires Transnational Comparable Data' , ibid, pp 59-75.
4 Boris Komarov, *The Destruction of Nature in the Soviet Union,* London, 1978; MG Khublaryan, 'Water Pollution and its consequences in the former USSR', in Schleicher, op cit.
5 Davies, 1992, op cit.
6 Richard North, *Death by Regualtion – The Butchery of the British Meat Industry,* London, IEA Health and Welfare Unit, 1993.
7 *Safer Eating,* Parliamentary Office of Science and Technology, 1997.
8 Ruth Brandon and Christie Davies, *Wrongful Imprisonment,* London: Allen and Unwin, 1973.
9 British Medical Association, op cit, p 129.
10 Davies, 1988, op cit; Green, 1987, op cit.
11 See Association of the British Pharmaceutical Industry *Pharma Facts and Figures,* London: ABPI, 1993.
12 Neal, op cit.
13 Ibid.
14 Max Weber, *The Protestant Ethic and the Spirit of Capitalism,* London: Unwin, 1930.
15 Karl Marx and Freidrich Engels, 'The German Ideology, Vol I Critique of Modern German Philosophy According to Its Representatives Feurbach, B Bauer and Stirner' In, Karl Marx, *Collected Works,* Vol V, London: Laurence and Wishart, 1976, p 47.
16 Christie Davies, 'Stupidity and rationality: jokes from the Iron Cage', in Chris Powell and George EC Paton (eds), *Humour in society, resistance and control.* London: MacMillan, 1988, pp 1-32.
17 The current malicious campaigns against fox hunting are nothing less than an attack on the culture and the way of life of people who live in rural or peripheral areas.
18 See L Altman and L Melcher, 'Fraud in Science', *British Medical Journal,* Vol 286, 1983, pp 2003-2006; M Angell and A S Relman, 'Fraud in Biomedical Research: A Time For Congressional Restraint', *New England Journal of Medicine,* Vol 38, 1988, pp 1463; W Broad and N Wade, *Betrayers of the Truth: Fraud and Deceit in the Halls of Science,* Oxford, OUP, 1985.
19 Philip Davies, *Organisational Development of Britain's Secret Intelligence Services 1969-1979,* unpublished PhD thesis, University of Reading, 1997.
20 This is a much more rational approach than trying to minimise pollution

regardless of the economic consequences.

21 See, Bryan Applyard, 'Hark, it's the great British whistle-blower', London: *The Sunday Times,* 1 June 1997, p 9; Greg Neale, 'New law will protect sex and safety whistle-blowers', London: *The Sunday Telegraph,* 5 October 1997.

22 Peter M Blau and Marshall W Meyer, *Bureacracy in Modern Society,* New York: Random House, 1987.

23 The chances of this happening are however slim. The present government seems intent in increasing regulation and protecting itself from criticism.

24 Brandon and Davies, op cit.

25 Michael Fumento, *The Myth of Heterosexual AIDS,* Chicago: Regrery, 2nd edn, 1993; Robert Root-Bernstein, *Rethinking AIDS: The Tragic Cost of Premature Consensus,* New York: The Free Press, 1993; BM Craven and GT Stewart, 'Public Policy and Public Health: Coping with potential medical disaster', in Roger Bate (ed), *What Risk?* Oxford, Butterworth Heinemann, 1997.

26 Digby Anderson, *A Diet of Reason: sense and nonsense in the healthy eating debate,* London: SAU, 1986.

27 Reiner Luyken, 'Die Protest-Maschine', *Die Zeit,* 37, 9, 6 September 1996; Wolfgang Mantow and Jens Pocleus, *Die Ereignisse um Brent Spar in Deutschland,* Hamburg: Wolfgang Mantow Kommunikations-beratung, 1996.

28 Luyken, op cit; Mantow and Pocleus, op cit.

29 Peter Berger and Thomas Luckmann, *The Social Construction of Reality,* New York: Doubleday, 1966.

30 Karl Popper, *Realism and the aim of science,* London: Hutchinson, 1983.

31 Post-modernism has fragmented all these disciplines and made apparent a latent absurdity that was there all the time.

32 Nigel Hawkes, 'Experts at odds over dangers of eating red meat', *The Times,* 25 October 1997.

33 Wildavsky, 1995, op cit.

34 British Medical Association, op cit, p 47.

35 These ugly notices mean, 'Beware of Side Winds', 'Slow Down Now', and 'Welcome to England'.

36 William Petersen, 'On the Sub-Nations of Western Europe', in Nathan Glazer and Daniel P Moynihan (eds), *Ethnicity, Theory and Experience,* Cambridge Mass Harvard University Press, 1975, pp 177-208.

37 Neal, op cit.

The Social Affairs Unit

The SAU is an independent research and educational trust committed to the promotion of lively and wide-ranging debate on social affairs. Its authors — over 200 — have analyzed the factors which make for a free and orderly society in which enterprise can flourish. It is committed to international co-operation in ideas: eg *The Loss of Virtue* and *This Will Hurt* published as **National Review Books**, *Gentility Recalled* published in co-operation with the Acton Institute and joint Anglo-European projects on food and alcohol policy. Current areas of work include consumer affairs, the critical appraisal of welfare and public spending and problems of freedom and personal responsibility.

The Unit's impact and funding

The Times (London) writes:

The Social Affairs Unit is famous for driving its coach and horses through the liberal consensus, scattering intellectual picket lines as it goes. It is equally famous for raising questions which strike most people most of the time as too dangerous or too difficult to think about.

To maintain its independence, the Unit is funded by a wide range of foundations and trusts, sales of its publications and corporate donations from highly diverse sectors. It has received support from well over 100 sources. The SAU is registered as an educational charity, number 281530.

The Social Affairs Unit

Suite 5/6 1st Floor

Morley House

Regent Street

London W1R 5AB

SOME PUBLICATIONS FROM THE SOCIAL AFFAIRS UNIT

On health and lifestyle...

The Death of Humane Medicine and the Rise of Coercive Healthism
Petr Skrabanek
ISBN 0 907631 59 2   £12.95

A New Diet of Reason: Healthy eating and government policy 1985–1995
David Conning
ISBN 0 907631 64 9   £5.00

Take a Little Wine — or Beer or Whisky — for Your Stomach's Sake
Digby Anderson
ISBN 0 907631 60 6   £5.00

Preventionitis: the exaggerated claims of health promotion
edited by James Le Fanu
ISBN 0 907631 58 4   £9.95

Health, Lifestyle and Environment: Countering the Panic
Published in co-operation with the Manhattan Institute
ISBN 0 907631 44 4   £9.95

A Diet of Reason: sense and nonsense in the healthy eating debate
edited by Digby Anderson
.Casebound: ISBN 0 907631 26 6
£9.95
Paperback: ISBN 0 907631 22 3
£5.95

Drinking to Your Health: The allegations and the evidence
edited by Digby Anderson
ISBN 0 907631 37 1   £14.95

On personal responsibility...

Loyalty Misplaced: misdirected virtue and social disintegration
edited by Gerald Frost
ISBN 0 907631 70 3   £12.95

Gentility Recalled: 'mere' manners and the making of social order
edited by Digby Anderson
Published in co-operation with the Acton Institute
ISBN 0 907631 66 5   £15.95

This Will Hurt: the restoration of virtue and civic order
edited by Digby Anderson
A NATIONAL REVIEW BOOK
ISBN 0 907631 63 0   £15.95

The Loss of Virtue: moral confusion and social disorder in Britain and America
edited by Digby Anderson
A NATIONAL REVIEW BOOK
ISBN 0 907631 50 9   £15.95

The Unmentionable Face of Poverty: domestic incompetence, improvidence and male irresponsibility in low income families
Digby Anderson
ISBN 0 907631 42 8   £4.00

Why Social Policy Cannot be Morally Neutral: the current confusion about pluralism
Basil Mitchell
ISBN 0 907631 35.5   £3.50

Self-Improvement and Social Action
Antony Flew
ISBN 0 907631 36 3   £3.50

A full list of publications is available on request